PRAISE FOR...

UNDERSTANDING THE PURPOSE AND POWER OF MEN

Male maturity does not come with age; it comes with the acceptance of responsibility. One of the greatest barriers to the maturation process is a man's failure to resolve his identity crisis. Dr. Munroe succinctly addresses that crisis by giving a clear definition of man and his role in human society. By pointing to man's origin, Dr. Munroe brings clarity to a man's true purpose and destiny. A book for men that women ought to read, too.

DR. A. R. BERNARD
PASTOR
CHRISTIAN CULTURAL CENTER
NEW YORK, NEW YORK

As one who has been enriched through the teachings and writings of Dr. Myles Munroe, I find the message in this book both significant and challenging. Dr. Munroe helps us to see that the problem facing men worldwide is not a biological one of maleness, but a spiritual one of identity. This book also helps us to rediscover the male's underlying purpose and gives us the principles for making that assessment.

This is an on-time and end-time book, not just to read, but to be used as a reference in charting our course for a better society and a richer life.

DR. BILL WINSTON
PASTOR
LIVING WORD CHRISTIAN CENTER
FOREST PARK, IL

Christian Business Network is currently leading a collaborative Fatherhood Initiative with community, state, and federal governmental leaders, focusing on the skyrocketing crisis of urban fatherless homes. Dr. Myles Munroe's leadership approach regarding what it means to be a man has once again helped us evaluate the conflicting signals government programmatic systems have caused through statistical data. *Understanding the Purpose and Power of Men* must be the model used to help eliminate the $150 billion per year that federal and state governments spend to subsidize and sustain single parent families.

This book helps males understand what it means to be a man, husband, and father so they can become change agents towards rebuilding families, communities, and ultimately a nation.

MR. JEROME EDMONDSON
PRESIDENT AND FOUNDER
CHRISTIAN BUSINESS NETWORK, INC.
SOUTHFIELD, MI

UNDERSTANDING

the Purpose and Power of

DR. MYLES MUNROE

w
WHITAKER
HOUSE

Editorial note: Even at the cost of violating grammatical rules, we have chosen not to capitalize the name satan and related names.

UNDERSTANDING THE PURPOSE AND POWER OF MEN

Dr. Myles Munroe
Bahamas Faith Ministries International
P.O. Box N9583
Nassau, Bahamas
e-mail: bfmadmin@bahamas.net.bs
web site: www.bfmmm.com

ISBN: 0-88368-725-9
Printed in the United States of America
© 2001 by Dr. Myles Munroe

Whitaker House
30 Hunt Valley Circle
New Kensington, PA 15068

Library of Congress Cataloging-in-Publication Data

Munroe, Myles.
  Understanding the purpose and power of men / by Myles Munroe.
     p. cm.
  ISBN 0-88368-725-9 (pbk. : alk. paper)
  1. Men (Christian theology) 2. Sex role—Religious
aspects—Christianity. I. Title.
  BT703.5 .M86 2002
  261.8'3431—dc21

                                   2001007727

   3 4 5 6 7 8 9 10 11 12 13 14 / 10 09 08 07 06 05 04 03 02

DEDICATION

To my beloved son, Chairo, with a hope that the content and principles of this book will become the quality of your character and the story of your life.

To Paul, forever my brother in this life and the next. May your memory live on through the things you taught me as a real male-man.

To my beloved dad, Matt Munroe—my male mentor.

To the men of BFM Fellowship's Real Men Ministry—your passion for truth inspires.

To males of every race, culture, creed, and nation in your struggle to discover and master the mystery of being a man.

To the Third-World man in his pursuit to recover his lost identity.

To the Manufacturer of the man and the male.

Acknowledgments

Our natural conception and birth is a result of human cooperation and established the priority the Creator places on our dependency on others for success and personal progress. This work is a testimony to this cooperation and confirms the reality that we are a sum total of all the contributions made to our lives by the people we have had the privilege to encounter on the journey of life. I am deeply grateful for the inspiration and wisdom of the men and women, both past and present, who, through their lives, instructions, corrections, challenges, commitment, and example, stirred gifts within me that I did not know I had.

I am also grateful to all the friends and colleagues of the International Third World Leaders Association who continue to inspire me to make a contribution to my generation and those to come.

For the development and production of this book itself, I feel a deep sense of gratitude to:

My precious wife, Ruth, and our children, Charisa and Chairo (Myles, Jr.), for their patience and support during my globe-trotting duties. Being your husband and father tested the reality of the principles in this book and has made me a real male-man. I love you all.

Lois Smith Puglisi, diligent and gifted editor and advisor, who shepherded this book from conception to its present form. You are a gift to any author, and may your gift continue to make a way for you in the world.

Jim Rill, for believing in me and the value of this message while patiently pursuing me to keep to the schedule and meet deadlines in completing this work.

CONTENTS

PREFACE

The twenty-first century male is in crisis. Throughout the nations of our global village, the prisons are filled with multitudes of men. Compared to their counterpart, women, they are responsible for a vast majority of the criminal behavior worldwide. They are also victims of drug abuse and the principal carriers of the dreaded AIDS virus. Many have found a home in subculture gangs, instigating antisocial activities that wreak havoc on the social order. Men revel in the oppression of women and perpetuate domestic violence.

In every culture and social system, men are struggling to find their place in a fast-changing world. In many societies, the dramatic change in the status of women, the workplace, and traditional cultural roles has left a significant number of men confused, disillusioned, angry, frustrated, and traumatized. Yes, the male of this cyber-technical, Internet-driven, postmodern world is caught in a worldwide web of confusion. Men are in trouble but are afraid to admit it. They are lost in a maze of new paradigms and the uncharted waters of social and cultural convergence.

Change is often the source of uncertainty and a measure of fear and anxiety. For many, this type of fear is difficult to manage, and it causes varying reactions. Some negative reactions to change include denial, ignorance, isolation, anger, resistance, and resentment. These reactions can cause serious effects on the environment in which the change is taking place. The result can be oppression, suppression, violence, and the spirit of control.

A brief study of the behavior of the male-factor in many nations today, including yours, will reveal such reactions to cultural changes. The drastic transitions taking place in social structures and the shifting of long-held beliefs are destroying the defining lines and the very definitions of our lives. For the male in most societies and cultures, this redefinition is traumatic and has rendered many men without a clear definition of manhood, masculinity, and fatherhood.

The impact of the confusion on women, the family, and society is also frightening. Many women suffer the violence of angry men. Children are victims of abuse and resentment, and society bears the scars of social deterioration. Governments are helpless to respond to this phenomenon. They find their ideas, laws, and social programs ineffective in addressing it. Men are clearly in trouble.

So what is a man to do? The number one challenge to the male is his identity crisis. The average man is confused about his manhood, masculinity, and sexuality. He doesn't have a clear definition of what a man is supposed to be. Some men have confused their cultural, social, and traditional roles with the definition of manhood. However, this has proven to be one of the major causes of the problem because, as the roles change, so does a man's image of himself.

How do we measure a man? What is true manhood? How do you define masculinity? What is true male sexuality? What is the true purpose of the male in relation to the female? Is there a universal definition of manhood? Can it be attained? Where do we go to get this definition?

This book addresses answers to these critical questions from the perspective of the male. The purpose and role of the male in the scheme of human experience is explored through returning to the original process of his creation, based on the premise that no one knows the product like the manufacturer. No product can understand its identity by asking the customer, because only the manufacturer knows the original purpose and potential of his product. Therefore, it is imperative that the male rediscover his original purpose and understand his true potential, as well as gain a clear understanding of his principal function within the human family.

The male is the key to building strong, enduring social infrastructures, stable families, sane societies, and secure nations. It is critical that the subject of the male's crisis be a priority for men, women, and national governments, so that we can secure progressive social developments within the countries of the world. Let us begin our journey through the land of cultural confusion to rediscover the purpose and power of the real male.

INTRODUCTION

The male holds the key to the nations—and our nations are in crisis. As the man goes, so goes the family, society, and the world. The problem is, men don't have a clear idea of where they're going anymore. They are suffering from a lost sense of identity—and the consequences for their families, communities, and nations are far-reaching.

CONFLICTING VIEWS OF MANHOOD

Traditional male roles once gave men continuity and balance from generation to generation. Today, many men are questioning who they are and what roles they are to play in life. On the surface, they may be following customary life pursuits, such as working, marrying, and having a family. Yet they have an inner uncertainty about what it means to be a man, a husband, and a father.

MALES ARE SUFFERING A LOST SENSE OF IDENTITY.

What is causing this uncertainty? A major reason is that society is sending out conflicting signals about what it means to be a man. Traditional views of masculinity compete side by side with new ideas of manhood in the marketplace of ideas—each vying for supremacy.

A CLASH OF OLD AND NEW IDEAS

This contest of ideas is being played out as we absorb the vast social and political changes that have taken place over the last forty years. On both national and international levels, cultures and ideas are colliding. As a result, people are reevaluating what it means to be human, what it means to be a man or a woman, and what it means to be a country. Some of these developments are:

10

- the movement for women's equality,
- the exportation of Western culture in the world,
- the fall of Communism,
- the global marketplace,
- a growing interconnectedness between nations.

Whether worldwide or locally, our world is rapidly changing before our eyes, and the social transformation accompanying it can often be painful. The clash of old and new ideas has left many men perplexed and frustrated in regard to their identity. How do their new roles (for example, equal partnership with women) play out against more traditional ones (such as breadwinner and protector)? Men are feeling compelled to redefine their roles as they attempt to adapt to these changing social expectations. This adjustment is disrupting both their professional and personal lives. It is altering their relationships with women. It is transforming family life.

Yet the lines of these new roles look blurry to men as traditional and contemporary ideas eclipse—overshadowing one another—and then separate again. For example, on the one hand, men are told there is no real difference between males and females and that they are to consider women as equals. On the other hand, they are encouraged to treat women with special care and courtesy—but when they do, they are often accused of chauvinism.

THE MALE IN CRISIS

Historically, men have defined their manhood by the various roles they have fulfilled for their families and for society. Now that these roles are in transition, they don't have a solid definition of masculinity to give them a cultural context for life. As a result, many men believe they have lost part of themselves, but they don't have anything concrete with which to replace it. Often, they don't even feel wanted or needed by women any longer. They used to have clear direction about where they were going as men. Now, it's as if they're trapped in a maze, frustrated and unable to move forward purposefully in life.

Some men have reacted angrily against the women's movement and other social changes. They have no intention of adapting. Instead, they have re-asserted or tightened their traditional dominance over women because they are afraid of losing control. They have re-acted by being either competitive or iso-lationist. They are domineering or even abusive to their families. In certain countries, men have aggressively fought back on a national level. They have countered the advancement of women's equality with severe restrictions on the lifestyle and freedoms of women because they perceive these changes to be part of the Westernization of their societies—a moral corruption that is harming their way of life.

MEN HAVE DEFINED THEIR MANHOOD BY THEIR ROLES.

A CRUCIAL CROSSROADS

Why is the male's crisis of purpose such a pivotal issue? For one thing, it attacks the core of who men are, leaving them indecisive and foundationally weak. For another, it reflects a breakdown in understanding, communication, and cooperation between men and women that is unnatural and unhealthy. Males are at a crucial crossroads, and where they go from here will have a serious effect on the course of society. The crisis of purpose they are experiencing will escalate if they continue to live in an uncertain or defensive state of mind. They will remain frustrated and will live at a level far below their potential. Moreover, the cracks in the foundation of society will grow dangerously wider.

What should men do? Should they hold on to traditional roles and ways of thinking, or should they follow the road being paved by new concepts of maleness?

It would be difficult to stop the flow of change, and we would not want to return to tradition merely for the sake of tradition. The old system did not reflect the full purpose and potential of men, and women were often devalued under it.

Yet contemporary concepts of maleness are often ambiguous. They also tend to focus on roles rather than on the male's underlying purpose and identity (a crucial distinction that this book explores). What kind of world will we have if we keep following this new path? We already have some idea of the negative effects that a continuing male crisis of purpose would bring. Many of our current social problems, such as teenage pregnancy, crime, and poverty, flow from purposelessness and rootlessness among men.

The majority of crimes worldwide are committed by men. Ninety to ninety-five percent of those in prison in the United States are males. Recently, I have been amazed at the increasing numbers of boys who are involved in crime. We are seeing more and more criminal activity by males between the ages of nine and eighteen. In London, a five-year-old boy was murdered by an eleven-year-old boy. In Chicago, a six-year-old girl was murdered by a nine-year-old boy. I remember when criminals used to be old men.

How often do you see a list of crimes that were committed during a given week in which 50 percent of the culprits were women? Never. It's really a male issue.

Whether we're talking about a broken home, an abused wife, an abandoned child, or a crime, we are looking primarily at a male problem that stems from a misguided purpose or a lack of true identity.

THE ISSUE IS PURPOSE, NOT MALENESS

Why are many social ills caused by men? It may be tempting for some to dismiss males as hopelessly aggressive and domineering, with an essential nature in need of an overhaul. I'd like to present an alternative perspective: the problem is not a biological one of *maleness*—but a spiritual one of *identity*. Male identity is not essentially a matter of *roles,* which vary with culture and shift with changing times—it is a matter of *inherent purpose.*

Therefore, to address the problems of our society and the world, we must start with the male and how he perceives himself. If men knew who they really are and their true reason for being, then their confusion, anger, and destructive behavior could be replaced with purposefulness, confidence, and a building up of society. It's when men don't know who they are and what purpose they have in this world that we experience a myriad of cultural problems.

While society is feeling the effects of the male's dilemma, it is also apparently contributing to it by presenting incomplete or confusing ideas of manhood. In this way, society is unknowingly bringing trouble upon itself. This double-edged sword is not new to our generation or our world.

THE CONSEQUENCES OF IGNORANCE OF PURPOSE

The crisis we are seeing today is actually a contemporary version of an age-old dilemma. Men and women alike lost their concept of what it truly means to be human— male and female—a long time ago. The problem is also not confined to particular cultures. The question of identity is a global problem. I have traveled to many nations, and I have concluded that most of the world is suffering from what I call the "consequences of ignorance of purpose." In every nation, in every community, no matter what language the citizens speak or what color their skin is, people are experiencing a common dilemma. They are suffering the debilitating effects of a misconception of purpose. They don't understand who they really are and therefore aren't living up to their full potential in life.

In my earlier book, *Understanding the Purpose and Power of Woman,* I showed how humanity's ignorance of purpose has historically degraded women. (I recommend that book to men, just as I recommend this one to women.) I talked about how we can alleviate the pain and unfulfilled potential this misunderstanding of purpose has caused women over the centuries so they can be free to become all they were meant to be.

However, neither males nor females will ever be fully actualized if the crisis of the male is not addressed, since men have a primary influence on the tone and direction of society. This influence is meant to be used for good. However, as we saw in regard to many of the social problems we are facing, it can have exactly the opposite effect if it's not understood or if it's abused. There is no way that we can have a safe and productive world as long as humanity as a whole doesn't know its reason for existence—and men in particular don't have a clear idea of their identity.

People can go for years without realizing they aren't fulfilling their true purpose. Both individuals and cultures can become comfortable following established roles without questioning their validity. However, our socially turbulent society is forcing us to examine the underlying foundation of our concepts of maleness and femaleness. In this sense, we can look at this crisis as a powerful opportunity for self-discovery and self-actualization. It is up to us to make accurate tests of the soundness of both traditional and contemporary ideas of what it means to be male and female, and then to relay a strong foundation for society.

OUR CRISIS OF IDENTITY IS A POWERFUL OPPORTUNITY FOR FINDING TRUE PURPOSE.

The purpose of this book is to give us principles for making that assessment and fulfilling our true purpose as human beings.

A REDISCOVERY OF PURPOSE

Therefore, to rediscover the masculine identity, we need to address these questions:

- How can men gain their footing in the ever-shifting environment of cultural expectations?
- What does it mean to be male?
- What definition of masculinity should men adopt?
- Why is a male's self-concept so important to the foundation of society?
- What roles should men fulfill—in the workplace and in the home?
- What do gender roles have to do with the male's purpose?

- What are the differences between males and females?
- How are men and women meant to relate to one another?
- How can a man build a better life for himself, his family, and the world?

In the following pages, I will explore these questions in a very straightforward and practical way. Join me for a rediscovery of purpose: the man as he was meant to be.

1

WHAT IS A REAL MAN?

MEN NEED A GOD-GIVEN IDENTITY IF THEY ARE TO FULFILL THEIR TRUE PURPOSE.

I magine that you are watching a television show similar to *To Tell the Truth*. Several contestants try to convince you that they are the Real Man. You have to guess which one is authentic and which ones are the imposters.

Contestant #1 tells you he is the Real Man because he fills the traditional male role: he supports his family financially while his wife cares for the children and the home. As long as he provides a roof over their heads and food for them to eat, he's fulfilling his duty as a husband and father. This man doesn't consider his wife to be his true equal.

Contestant #2 says he is the Real Man because he has a culturally progressive role: he shares household and child-rearing responsibilities with his wife while they both pursue careers. He thinks of his wife as his equal.

Contestant #3 explains that he is the Real Man because he has been freed from male stereotypes and has decided to take on the nurturer role of caring for the children and home while his wife goes to work. He considers his wife equal to himself—or maybe even better, since she has a more compassionate, sensitive nature than he does.

These are some of the images of manhood that are competing for men's acceptance today. Many men feel as if they're being asked to guess what a real man is by determining which "contestant" has the most convincing facial expressions and answers. Yet there seems to be no clear-cut winner. In addition, society keeps mixing and matching these images until men don't know what's expected of them anymore. They are confused and frustrated as they try to sort through their own expectations for manhood while feeling pressure from the various segments of society that are promoting these images—or an impossible combination of them. Meanwhile, Hollywood is flooding society with intriguing icons of masculinity, such as James Bond and Rambo. Even though these images are superheroes rather than real men, it's sometimes hard to escape their allure. It's difficult not to start thinking that a real man should somehow imitate the power and resourcefulness they exhibit.

A CRISIS OF ROLES

What makes our current cultural situation unsettling for men is that males have traditionally defined their manhood by their roles: the functions they perform for their families and in society. However, there's been a major shift in the roles of both males and females. The rules of society are changing. This has happened just in the last forty years or so. We're in the middle of a cultural transition, and competing ideas of masculinity are causing perplexing problems for men. They are being pulled in several directions at once while they try to figure out what it means to be a real man in today's world.

THE ROLES AND THE RULES OF SOCIETY ARE CHANGING.

In recent years, literature focusing on changes in men's lives has indicated that the male is in a state of crisis and internal conflict. An array of studies are telling us that males aren't quite sure who they are or what women expect from them. Without a clear idea of their identity, men are trying to cope with the collision of new societal expectations and traditional ideas of what a man should be, which they have internalized through family, culture, or natural inclination.

Men's basic conceptions of manhood are therefore being disrupted. They feel displaced. They are either frustrated and struggling to adapt to a new but vague concept of who they are, or they're angry and trying to reverse the flow of change.

Are traditional roles to be totally abandoned? If so, what will replace them? Many men have unanswered questions, such as these:

1. *Is a man still supposed to be the breadwinner and protector?* Today, the woman goes out and makes her own bread and says she doesn't need protection. A man isn't sure what he's supposed to do for a woman anymore.

2. *Is a man still the leader and authority in the home?* This isn't clear anymore. The woman says, "You're not my authority. I'm not a slave. I make my own money and my own decisions. I do what I want to. I'll call you when I'm ready for you." A man doesn't know how he's supposed to relate to a woman any longer.

3. *Should a man still show chivalry?* Should he open the door for a woman, escort her, pay for her meal on a date, and so on? A man will pull out a chair for a woman and she'll say, "That's all right. Thank you very much, but I'll pull my own chair out." Sometimes a man will open a door for a woman and she'll be offended. "Do you think I'm crippled?" she'll demand. If a woman walks into a room and a man stands up out of respect, she might look at him as if he's crazy. A man isn't sure if he should be nice to a woman anymore.

4. *Is a man still the defender of his family, property, and country?* More women are entering law enforcement and the armed forces and are carrying guns. Some men don't know how to react to these changes. A woman walks into the house with her uniform on and her husband is scared to say hello to her. He'll jump up and say, "Sergeant!" Many men are thinking, "She really doesn't require me to protect her." Men don't know if women even need them anymore.

Is there anything now that marks a man as different from his female counterpart? Based on the above scenarios, that's a difficult question to answer. Males and females are in a state of gender upheaval and confusion.

So what do you do in order to be a man in the twenty-first century? Who are men in relation to women? How are men to sort out the various versions of masculinity that are being promoted in the world?

If you are a male and feel that your work, your relationships, and your view of the world are being turned upside down, you're not alone. This is the most complex time in the world to be a man. Men of all ages are grappling with competing views and values of manhood.

What has happened?

THOUSANDS OF YEARS OF TRADITION SET ASIDE

Males used to acquire their ideas of manhood from observing their fathers or from longstanding cultural traditions. There was a continuity of masculine roles from generation to generation. Things are different now. Hundreds, even thousands, of years of tradition have been set aside in just one or two generations. This shift may have started in Western and industrialized nations with the women's movement and other cultural changes, but its influence is being felt in one way or another all over the world.

MEN AND WOMEN HAD SPECIFIC ROLES THAT DID NOT OVERLAP.

For example, my life is completely different from my father's life. I can't use the way my father did things as a model for myself, and my sisters can't use the environment in which my mother functioned as an example for themselves. Our parents lived not only in a different generation, but also with different concepts of maleness and femaleness. Historically speaking, until recently, the man had certain accepted roles and the woman had certain accepted roles, and they didn't usually overlap.

HISTORICAL ROLES

You can go back fifty, one hundred, five hundred, two thousand, four thousand years, and you'll find a fairly consistent pattern of roles for men and women that were acknowledged and valued. There were some very practical reasons for this longstanding pattern. There have always been certain exceptions to the pattern among individuals and cultures, but the following is the way most families conducted themselves for generations. This traditional pattern continues to have an influence on male-female relationships today.

THERE WAS A BIOLOGICAL DETERMINATION OF ROLES

In pre-modern times, biology contributed largely to the roles of men and women. Males are generally physically stronger than women, so the men were the ones who went out to hunt and provide for the family. Females are biologically equipped to have babies, so they cared for the children. In general, there were no birth control options and no abortion alternatives with which a woman could supersede biology. A man didn't have to wonder whether he or his wife would stay home and raise the children. Roles were less complicated because they were predetermined by biology.

EVERYDAY LIVING WAS A STRUGGLE FOR SURVIVAL

In addition, people lived in a more hostile physical environment in which day-to-day living was a struggle for survival. This was another reason why the man, who was physically stronger, naturally became the provider and protector of the family.

At that time, making a living was an especially precarious job. The man literally had to risk his life to take care of his family. This caused his wife and children to look to him for leadership and to value his crucial contribution to their survival. They depended on him.

MEN HAD TO RISK THEIR LIVES MAKING A LIVING.

When a man went out to get food for his family, there was no guarantee that he would come back alive. He might be fatally wounded by an animal or die of exposure. Therefore, the woman rejoiced to see him come home again. The

21

same basic attitude held true in our parents' and grandparents' time when most husbands were the sole breadwinners of their families and their wives stayed at home. In the evening, the whole family was happy that the father had returned. Why? He had been out there in a risky world trying to make a living. Sometimes jobs were hard to come by. Sometimes the only job a man could get was working long hours in the fields or underground in a coal mine. When a man came home limping, his wife knew he had risked his health or even his life to keep bread on the table.

The family that I grew up in was a typical family of the not-so-distant past. I am one of eleven children. My father rose in the morning before we children got up, and he came home after we had gone to bed. He spent his whole life working, trying to feed almost a dozen children, keeping a roof over our heads and clothes on our backs. It was a twenty-four-hour-a-day job. My mother had to stay home, and her job was as hard as his. She had to take care of all eleven of us—cooking the meals, bathing us, washing our clothes, getting us off to school, making sure we did our homework, disciplining us. It was a very hard life. It was survival.

ROLES AND SKILLS BECAME ESTABLISHED

The basic needs of survival required men and women to develop specific roles and skills, which were passed along to succeeding generations. Up until your grandparents' time or even your parents' time, everybody knew his or her role and had skills that were equal to it. The husband knew what he needed to do, and he did it; the wife knew what she had to do, and she did it.

In this way, although survival was difficult, relationships were comparatively easy because there was no confusion over gender roles. A man and a woman didn't have to wonder whether one was infringing on the other's territory. Her role was to keep the house, cook the food, and care for the children. His job was to hunt or harvest the crops and build a dwelling in order to provide food and shelter for the family.

Life was straightforward and so, in that sense, relationships were less complicated.

INTERDEPENDENCE CREATED A NATURAL APPRECIATION

This partnership in survival produced an interdependence between men and women that generated a mutual appreciation. Because they both worked so hard and did their individual parts, they respected one another. It was a natural appreciation. It was natural because their roles were very clear and were accepted as necessary and important.

In many of these marriages, there wasn't the kind of relationship between husband and wife that we know today. The man was motivated by simple things: food, sex, children, and security. He was not motivated by conversation and sentimental exchange, by emotional and psychological sensitivity. He came home when he wanted to meet basic needs.

For the most part, a man was honored and loved by his wife not because he was a good man or an affectionate companion, but because she knew he risked his life to take care of her and the children. She loved him because of what he did for her. He didn't earn her honor and appreciation because he was a sentimental, romantic guy. She valued his provision. If he didn't brave the elements and come back with fresh meat, she wouldn't respect him.

SURVIVAL MODE DIDN'T LEAVE TIME FOR ROMANCE.

The woman spent time nurturing the children and creating a home, and she was respected and loved by the man for her contribution to the family. He didn't necessarily honor her because she was charming or because "the Word of God says to do so." He honored her because she bore his children and because he knew the value of the work that she was doing. He didn't worry about who was going to feed and clean the children or who was going to wash their clothing. His wife did all that, and he respected her for it.

This means that romance was not a significant part of the lives of many of our early forefathers. They were too busy trying to survive. When you're in survival mode, there isn't much time for sentiment.

It was much the same way for many married couples up until the relatively recent past. A man spent all day working. He was occupied with providing for and protecting his family. He didn't have time for romance when he came home. All he wanted was food and sex. He wasn't concerned about taking his wife out to dinner or on shopping outings or giving her money to spend. He had money only to survive. The relationship was simply, "Look, we have to survive and I have to protect you. Whatever I have to do to accomplish these things, that's life."

The man thought of his marriage as a partnership, but partnership didn't mean the same thing then that it does to us today. He didn't consider his wife to be equal to him or as good as he was. Instead, partnership meant that she had her part to play and he had his part. Men and women were taught this concept of marriage. A husband and wife honored each other because of their individual contributions to the partnership, not because they acknowledged that there is an equality between men and women.

This is where we came from as a society. However, things have changed.

CONTEMPORARY ROLES

Life is completely different for men and women now because we are no longer utterly dependent on one another for security and survival. Our roles and strategies have really changed.

Men no longer have the job that they held almost exclusively for centuries. They used to have a role that was very clear—one they didn't share with their wives. How was manhood measured? Young men were told, "Get a job, son, so you can provide for your family, and have some babies." Being the breadwinner and having the ability to procreate was the measure of a man. But the way society views men is in transition, and these are not considered the primary marks of manhood any longer. A number of families still follow the traditional pattern of the husband holding the job while the wife stays home with the children, especially while the children are young. However, even these marriages are usually influenced by contemporary rather than traditional ideas of how men and women are to relate to one another.

BIOLOGY IS NO LONGER AS GREAT A FACTOR

Biology doesn't determine male-female roles and functions the way it used to. Today, because of the prevalence of both dual careers and birth control, a husband and wife might choose not to have children. Also, because of the widespread idea that fertility is a woman's business alone, the woman will often tell the man when or if they will have a baby. Even if they do have a child, that doesn't necessarily mean that the wife will stay home to take care of the baby all day or every day. Daycare and other childcare options enable her to work at a job outside the home either part-time or full-time.

This change is bringing new kinds of stresses to the family. If daycare workers or nannies are bringing up the children, sometimes the children don't really know their parents. Also, the parents don't always know what the baby-sitter is doing or teaching the children while they are at work. Essentially, this means that the children are being brought up by people whom the parents cannot be sure of.

In addition, since a woman's childbearing and child-rearing was what formerly brought her respect from her husband, the man now has to find another way to honor his wife. Because of the traditional pattern, when a wife demands respect from her husband today, he sometimes thinks, "Well, what are you doing to earn it?"

Twenty-first century relationships are difficult.

WE ARE NO LONGER IN SURVIVAL MODE

Most of us don't focus on survival and protection the way people used to. This is not to say that we don't face economic challenges and job-related stress, but the physical risk is not the same. We're not out hunting food and facing the elements just to stay alive. We have twenty-four-hour-a-day grocery stores and microwave ovens. While we live in an uncertain world where there are still dangers, the physical environment is much friendlier now than it was for our forefathers. Today, a man will leave the house in the morning dressed in his three-piece suit as he drives his Lexus to work—as a doctor in a fancy office. The physical risk is gone for most people.

One of the differences between the old and the new ways is that, when people get married, they often already have most of what they need, instead of having to struggle for it. Moreover, the woman is no longer dependent on the man to provide for her after they marry. Because the traditional role of provider is ingrained in many men, this situation can be unsettling to a man.

For example, a man will meet a woman and discover that she already owns material possessions. Because she has been working for a while, she makes more money than **WHAT CAN A** he does and drives an expensive car. She **MAN OFFER** owns a condominium, a thirty-five inch **A WOMAN** television, a refrigerator, and the food in **TODAY?** it. She can buy her own gas for her car. She has it all worked out, and then he says he wants to marry her and take care of her. How is she going to depend on him? She has money in the bank. What is the man going to give her? She isn't looking for survival and protection; she's independent, and so her expectations in regard to men and marriage are totally different.

Some women wonder, "How am I supposed to be submissive when I make more money than my husband, and the house and furniture are mine?" In other words, she's saying to the man, "You have to earn the right for me to submit to you by giving me something I haven't already given you." That's a tough statement for a man to hear. So the man says, "Well, I can't give you anything because you owned more than I did from the very beginning." How does a woman submit to somebody whom she believes she is supporting? It's a difficult situation for both men and women. But it's the world we live in.

Do you wonder why divorces are so common these days? One reason is that a woman can now tell a man straight and fast, "If you can't take care of this properly, I'm going to leave." My mother had eleven children. When she had a problem, she couldn't say to my father, "I'm going to leave you." Where was she going to go? She had no professional or academic training, no preparation for a job outside the home. The home was her life.

Independence is a relatively new situation for women, and men are still learning to cope with the change. In many ways, the woman has taken over not only the man's traditional role of provider, but also that of protector. She has mace, she has a gun in her purse, and she has a cell phone to call the police instantly. So what does the man do? He says, "I'm your protector," and she says, "I don't need you to protect me." It's a different world. Men don't know what they're supposed to do for women anymore.

WOMEN ARE BRINGING HOME NOT ONLY THE BACON BUT ALSO THE PIG!

ROLES AND SKILLS ARE LESS COMPARTMENTALIZED

Men and women used to exist in different spheres. A man's sphere was work and survival. The woman's world was the home and children. There was no confusion of roles. They knew exactly where they were supposed to be.

A woman leaving the home and entering the workplace means that the home is no longer kept by her specifically. The man isn't sure what his job in the home is, and the woman isn't sure what her job in the home is. They're confused.

Your father used to bring home the bacon, but now your wife is bringing home not only the bacon but the pig. Besides that, she owned two pigs before you married her. She doesn't want any bacon from you; she already has bacon.

If both husband and wife are now bringing home the bacon, then who's the provider? That's a problematic question for men. If both are paying the mortgage, then who's putting the roof over their heads? Your father was considered the owner of his house because he bought and paid for it. Today, the house doesn't belong to the man. It belongs to both the man and the woman.

Some men wonder how their fathers used to be the "man of the house." Now, if a man puts his foot down, his wife will put her foot down, too. The things men were taught no longer work. Your father says, "Put her in her place." You say, "But the place belongs to her." "Show her who wears the pants in the family." "But she wears pants, too!"

Many couples face difficult economic situations that require both of them to work to make ends meet. However, the cultural shift of women going to college, pursuing careers, and delaying marriage has made significant changes in family life.

For example, a man may say, "Honey, you have to bring up the children," and she'll say, "No, I'm going to work." "Why?" "I want to use my education, and I want a certain standard of living that requires a double salary, so I'm going to work." He says, "But who will bring up the kids? You are the child-bearer and the child-nurturer." Her answer is, "My employer has a daycare center. I'm taking the job."

What does a man do when his wife makes more money than he does, and he believes he's supposed to be the provider and protector of the home? He's frustrated and even ashamed. That's one of the reasons why there's so much quarreling in our modern marriages. We keep arguing over who's supposed to do what.

These and other similar situations have changed our perspectives dramatically and altered our traditional roles. The male isn't sure what a man is anymore, and the female isn't sure what a woman is anymore. This change has caused tension for women as well as men.

For instance, some woman actually feel guilty when they say, "I'm a homemaker." Do you think that in your parents' or grandparents' time, people asked a woman, "So, what do you do?" The question never came up. But today, almost every woman is asked what she does. In other words, we know what she *doesn't* do. She doesn't just stay home and bring up children—with the implication that this is something to be ashamed of.

It used to be much easier for the woman who stayed at home with her children. She had support in this role because every woman in the neighborhood was at home. Today, people think something is wrong with a woman if she is a homemaker. They think things like: "What's the matter with her? Is she lazy?" or "She's not very creative," or "She must not be smart enough to have a career," or "She needs to get a life." The idea is being promoted in society that "only dumb women stay home."

The results of changing gender roles can be distressing for both men and women. People are confused about how to act in this new world. It has become a psychological dilemma for them. Many are feeling tense and displaced, and they are trying to figure out what is wrong with them. I'll tell you right now what is wrong: it's simply a different world.

INDEPENDENCE HAS CHANGED THE PARAMETERS OF APPRECIATION

Increasingly independent, self-sufficient, contemporary women no longer feel the need for men to provide for and protect them. This is a problem for men. They're trying to get along in a relationship, and they're not sure who is responsible for what. For example, a boy takes a girl out for lunch, and he looks at her and says, "Are you going to pay for yours?" Thirty years ago, the man automatically paid. Why? It was the man's job to be the provider. But now if a man takes a woman to dinner, and he finds he doesn't have enough money, she reaches into her purse and says, "I'll make up for it." He feels shame, but she's not ashamed, because she has the money. And guess what? She still likes him. She likes him because she feels there aren't too many good men around anyway.

The independence of women is diminishing men's traditional value to them. Historically, men have always died at an earlier age than women. Why? They had to go out into the cold and sleet in the winter, even if they were coughing with tuberculosis, in order to provide for the family. They were the sole element of survival for the family. This is why women valued them. Sometimes, when a women reveals that her husband is abusing her, and she's asked, "Why don't you leave him?" she'll reply, "I can't do that." That's a deep answer. There are certain things about him she values.

If a man spent every day risking his life to protect you and the children and to provide for you, then how are you going to feel about him? Obviously, you are going to esteem him highly, because you know what he's doing to take care of the family. That is why it was natural for your mother, even when your father didn't always act right, to love and honor him. He was valuable to her.

Today, however, this is not necessarily the case. When a man shows interest in a woman, she may tell him, "Now, let me tell you this right up front: if you can't cut the mustard, you can leave whenever you're ready. And if we get married, I want you to sign a prenuptial agreement so that everything I bring into the marriage will stay mine if the marriage ends." Women don't value

SOME MEN ARE AFRAID THAT THEIR WIVES DON'T NEED THEM.

men in the way that they used to because the needs men used to supply are now being supplied by the women themselves. Some husbands are afraid of their wives because they think their wives don't need them.

Another significant change is that, for the first time in recorded history, men and women look to one another primarily for love and companionship rather than survival and protection. Our priorities as human beings have changed. People are looking for something more in their relationships. Happiness, intimacy, and lasting passion are now requirements for a relationship. Yet understanding how to provide these things often does not come easy for a man.

HAPPINESS

The male's traditional roles are not enough to make his partner happy anymore. Women want companionship and attention in order to be happy. My father couldn't take my mother for walks or out to dinner at a restaurant. There was no time for it. He made my mother happy just by making sure that the family had clothing, running water, and so on.

What can men do to make women happy today? That's the challenge. Have you ever heard a man say, "What does a woman want?" In the past, men used to tell their wives, "Woman, what else do you want from me? I put a roof over your head and food in the kitchen." Remember when men said that? Those days are over.

INTIMACY

When the man risked his life to give his wife food and protection, then intimacy, sensitivity, and good communication skills were not an issue. The woman didn't say, "Honey, you have to learn the psychological and emotional instability of a woman going through menstruation." A man didn't have time to learn to get along with a woman. Again, when he arrived home, it was dark, he was tired, and all he wanted was food and sex. The house was his, the food was his, and the rationale was, "It's time to pay up."

THE CAVEMAN DIDN'T HAVE TIME TO LOOK AT HIS WIFE'S DRESS.

But nowadays, women want intimacy and communication. "Talk to me. You haven't told me you love me all day." That's the way women think today. "You looked at everybody else except me. You didn't notice my dress." Listen, the caveman didn't have time to look at any dress. He was too busy trying to survive. But the world has changed.

Did your parents or grandparents ever talk about PMS? They were probably too busy to talk about it, and people—even husbands and wives—weren't as open about such topics. Now, the social atmosphere has changed, and we have more time to think about these things. These days, a woman might say, "Don't touch me now; I'm going through my cycle. My hormones are out of balance." A man now has to study what "mood" his wife is in. When you're just trying to survive, you're not thinking in terms of moods. It wasn't necessarily a better way of life, but it was definitely a different way. Men are still trying to figure out how to build intimacy and communication into their relationships.

A woman may wonder why her husband has problems talking with her. He doesn't know what to say, and she doesn't realize what he's going through. For example, suppose she has a fantastic job—a leadership job, an administrative job—and he has a lesser job. She comes home and tries to talk to him at dinner. What do they talk about? She's conversing on a highly intellectual level, and he's not there yet, because his job doesn't require him to stretch that far. So she says a couple of sentences, and he's intimidated. He says to himself, "Oh, that's a big word she used." He doesn't know what to do, because his leadership role seems to have diminished.

In this challenging time in our culture, women need to show understanding to the men in their lives. For example, suppose a woman marries a man, and they are settled in their house, and she says to him, "Be a man." He says, "Okay...how?" His back is against the wall. He used to know what that meant, but not any longer. So she says things like, "Be my spiritual head." He looks at her blankly. "My father was a caveman. He taught me that the Bible and church are for weaklings. So I'm really not much into church. I'll go to please you, but if that makes me a man, it's going to take a while." He doesn't understand spiritual matters as well as she does because he was taught that religion is for women.

So she says, "Comfort me," and he says, "How?" He didn't receive that kind of training from his father. She says, "Show me affection," and he says, "Oh, no. How do you spell that?" She says, "Be sentimental," and he says, "Sentamen-who? What is that?" He doesn't understand what she means.

What do many women do in this situation? They become angry. "Just be a man!" "How?" "Provide for me!" "But you make more money than I do." The man is confused. He doesn't realize she wants him to provide for her emotional needs—or if he does understand, he doesn't know how to fulfill those needs. Men need patience and understanding from their wives.

Passion

Passion is also necessary for today's relationships.

Remember that, in the old days, the man would just ask, "Woman, are you ready or not?" There were no romantic preliminaries. He'd say, "Tarzan ready for Jane. Jane ready? Okay, bring it on." That was it.

Now, however, women want men to turn the lights down, bring scented candles into the room, and put flowers everywhere. The men say, "What's going on here?" You have to work for it now, men. It's hard work!

These days, women want men to start romancing them in the morning—make them breakfast, run the bathwater for them, take them out to lunch, call them five times to tell them they love them, pick them up in a limousine and take them out for a nice dinner—then they might be rewarded that night. There's no guarantee, but they won't be rewarded without working for it.

Male-Female Relationships Have Become a Mystery

In many aspects of life, therefore, the roles and relationships of men and women have completely changed in the last few decades. This putting aside of traditional male roles seems frightening and even dangerous to many men because they don't know where it leaves them. They feel there's now a great deal of mystery in the relationships between men and women, and **CONFUSION OVER PURPOSE WILL SIDELINE OR DESTROY PEOPLE'S LIVES.** they don't know what to expect. I can empathize with what they're going through. Studying this topic has made me realize that we're really in a cultural dilemma. I feel for men. They don't know what to do. If you are a woman, you need to understand that men are really in trouble.

I have tried to give you a picture of what changing gender roles have done to throw men off balance, so that you can see the nature of the dilemma they're facing. Some of the scenarios I've given are humorous, but the problems males are facing are serious because they have to do with purpose and identity. They are serious because confusion over purpose will sideline and even destroy people's lives.

ROLES VERSUS PURPOSE

All this ultimately comes down to what males use as a basis for their self-worth and identity. Because men have linked their identity to their roles, now that the roles have changed, they have left themselves no basis for manhood. Whatever they replace their old idea of masculinity with may or may not be a true or fulfilling role for them. What is more troubling, when men don't understand their place in the world, they will often either withdraw from it or use their influence in harmful ways, such as committing crimes.

What can men do to regain their footing and identity?

MEN MUST THINK IN TERMS OF PURPOSE RATHER THAN ROLES.

First, they must adopt an entirely new way of thinking. They need to think in terms of *purpose* rather than *roles*. The reason they are having problems today is that they have been basing their worth on the wrong thing all along. Roles have never been the true basis of a male's identity and purpose. Roles can be helpful or harmful, but ultimately they merely reflect culture and tradition.

What men really need to discover is their underlying purpose, which transcends culture and tradition. A man's position and actions must flow out of his purpose, not the other way around. That is why the answer to the male's dilemma is not just to adjust to changing times—although some of this will be needed—but to discover the inherent purpose of the male. Since we live in a confused society, the knowledge of what it means to be a true man cannot be acquired by observing the culture around us. Males need an understanding of themselves that is not overly influenced by societal trends—in short, by someone else's image of them. Where, then, can we go for answers?

One of the themes we'll keep returning to in this book is that the purpose of something can be found only in the mind of its maker. Men therefore need a God-given identity if they are to fulfill their true purpose. We must learn what God originally intended for them. To do this, we must go back and rediscover the Creator's original plan for both men and women.

Once more, we must realize that when men are ignorant of their true identity, it affects not only their own callings and fulfillment, but also that of their families and of society as a whole. This is because God has given males a unique leadership influence. As the man goes, so goes the family, society, and the world. I believe that if we don't address the male's identity crisis, our whole generation is in trouble. There's no escaping this fact.

The answer for males in the twenty-first century is therefore to—

- Define their worth based on God's purpose, rather than society's roles.
- Learn God's vision for their lives.
- Continue to live in the truth of who they were created to be.

If males understand the purpose and responsibilities God has given them and the true design of their relation-ship with females, they can be free to fulfill their destiny and potential. They can be the men they were created to be.

If you are a man, you don't need to be confused about your identity and place in life, regardless of the conflicting signals society is currently sending out. You will find fresh vision and direction in rediscovering God's purposes for both males and females. Through this knowledge, men can be and do more than they ever imagined, and women can gain a new understanding and appreciation for men while enabling them to fulfill their calling.

What is a "real man"? Someone who knows the reality of who he is and who lives in that reality. This knowledge starts with understanding the significance of being created purposefully by God.

PRINCIPLES

1. Males have traditionally defined their manhood by their roles.

2. Historically, men and women had established roles that didn't overlap.

3. Relationships are different for men and women now that we no longer depend on one another for security and survival.

4. Men are in a crisis of identity and purpose.

5. Confusion over purpose will sideline and even destroy a person's life.

6. If a man links his identity to his roles, when the roles change, he gives himself no basis for manhood.

7. A man's identity is found in his purpose, not in his roles.

8. Men's underlying purpose transcends culture and tradition.

9. Knowledge of what it means to be a true man cannot be acquired by observing the confused culture around us.

10. The purpose of something can be found only in the mind of its maker.

11. Men need a God-given identity if they are to fulfill their true purpose.

12. When men are ignorant of their true identity, it affects not only their own callings and fulfillment, but also that of their families and of society as a whole. This is because, as the man goes, so goes the family, society, and the world.

13. A real man is someone who knows the reality of who he is and who lives in that reality.

2

SEVEN PRINCIPLES
OF PURPOSE

GOD'S PURPOSE IS THE KEY TO OUR FULFILLMENT.

God desires that every man find his purpose and fulfill it. If a man wants to know who he is in order to live fully in that reality, he must first understand God's principles of purpose. He has to learn these anchors for living from the Word of God. Otherwise, he will fall into a trap of confusion—where many of us are right now.

Proverbs 19:21 is a foundational Scripture in regard to understanding God's purpose: *"Many are the plans in a man's heart, but it is the Lord's purpose that prevails."* This crucial truth tells us that we can make all the plans we want to in life, but if we don't make our plans according to the purposes for which God created us, then our plans will be in vain. We won't live up to our full potential, and we will be unfulfilled. We may even pursue goals and engage in practices that are harmful for us. We have only one life, and we have to make that life count if we are ever to fulfill our purpose.

HOW ARE YOU USING YOUR LIFE?

What value do you place on your life? Do you know that one of the most dangerous things in life is wasting time? It is said that time is a commodity that you never are able to recapture. Once you've lost time, it's gone forever. What you've lived, you can never relive. So the best thing to do with time is to use it in a way that will bring the greatest results. The best way—the only way—to use time effectively is to do *what* you are supposed to do *when* you are supposed to do it. Effectiveness does not mean just doing good things, but rather doing the right thing.

GOOD VERSUS BEST

It would be terrible to be busy doing the wrong things your entire life. Wouldn't it be sad to be serious and committed and faithful—to the wrong thing? It's possible to do what is good but not what is right. What I mean is this: it is possible to do good things but not the things that are best based on God's purposes for you. One of the devil's greatest weapons against my life is to get me busy doing things that are good but that are not right and best for me.

God created each of us with a purpose. That purpose is what's right for us. Suppose Jesus had become a priest in the Sanhedrin, the highest council and tribunal of the Jews. That would have been a good thing. Suppose He had become a member of the Sadducees and been one of the leaders in the social structure of Galilee and Judea. That would have been a good thing. Suppose He had become a social worker, helping the poor, having massive crusades, feeding multitudes of people every day with bread and fish. Would that have been a good thing? Sure. Suppose He had devoted every hour to healing the sick and raising the dead. That would have been a good thing, wouldn't it? Yet it would not have been the right thing for Him.

EFFECTIVENESS MEANS DOING WHAT YOU WERE MEANT TO DO.

There was a time when Jesus began to tell His disciples that He would be crucified. They didn't want to hear that. *"Peter took him aside and began to rebuke him. 'Never, Lord!' he said. 'This shall never happen to you!'"* (Matt. 16:22). The disciples' reaction to Jesus' purpose was, "We rebuke You. Get that thought out of Your mind. You will not die." But Jesus turned around and rebuked them for their shortsighted perspective. *"Jesus turned and said to Peter, 'Get behind me, Satan! You are a stumbling block to me; you do not have in mind the things of God, but the things of men'"* (v. 23). Jesus was saying, in effect, "I know why I was born. I know the purpose for My life. Don't distract Me with things that are merely good. I must pursue the highest purpose."

One of the reasons Jesus knew His purpose was that He was continually seeking God and in constant communication with Him. That is the pattern each of us needs to follow. Why? It's dangerous to live without God. If you don't know God, you'll never know your reason for existence. And if you don't know why you were born, you could live a completely wrong life. I didn't say a bad life. There are many good people who are pursuing relationships, careers, and goals in life that are not best for them. What we have to concern ourselves with is living effectively. The only way to live a fulfilled life is to know why you were born.

FULFILLING YOUR PURPOSE

Have you ever had a new car break down on you right in the middle of traffic? You got out and kicked one of the tires. You just wanted to curse at it because the car wasn't fulfilling its purpose. It was brand-new. It looked sleek. It had a nice paint job. But you couldn't drive it. What made you angry at the car? It's simple: the car's purpose was to transport you, to make you mobile; but the car was not taking you anywhere. No matter how great the car looked, it wasn't right; it wasn't fulfilling its purpose.

KNOWING AND FULFILLING YOUR PURPOSE IS THE ONLY WAY TO DO WHAT IS RIGHT.

Many men are like that car. They're stopped in the middle of traffic, and they don't even realize it. They're spending their lives doing things that look good, but they don't know God—or they know much too little about Him and His ways.

We have to realize that good deeds are not a substitute for rightness. Knowing and fulfilling your purpose is the only way to do what is right. Remember our foundational verse: *"Many are the plans in a man's heart, but it is the Lord's purpose that prevails"* (Prov. 19:21). One of the reasons why this verse is so important is that many people are planning to use charitable work as their ticket into heaven. It's very dangerous to attempt to bribe God. God is not impressed with all the good things we do. He's waiting for us to do what He's asked us to do in the first place.

Discovering our purpose enables us to stop wasting our lives and start fulfilling our potential. However, then we must be careful not to become sidetracked along the way. The greatest way to destroy someone is to distract the person from his or her true purpose. Sometimes people will do this unintentionally, as we saw from the example of Peter and Jesus. However, whether people try to distract us out of the best or worst of intentions, we must learn to remain steadfast in the purpose for which we were created.

REMAINING CONSTANT IN YOUR PURPOSE

Nehemiah fulfilled an important purpose in life, but he might have been persuaded to be sidetracked. He was in exile serving as cupbearer to the king of Persia when he heard that the city of Jerusalem was still in a broken-down condition. He was distressed over this news and determined, "I've got to repair the city." So he prayed, and then he obtained permission from the king to rebuild the wall of Jerusalem. God's favor was on his plans because this was the purpose for which he was created. He went and started to rebuild the wall with the help of the remnant of Jews in Jerusalem.

However, some men from the surrounding area didn't like what Nehemiah was doing, and they tried to stop him. They ridiculed and slandered him, but he kept on with the work. They conspired to kill him, but he armed some of the workers with weapons and thwarted the plot. They tried to fill him with fear and make him flee for his life. One of the last things they tried is usually the most effective means of sidetracking people. They said, "Come, let's have a meeting; let's discuss what you're doing. Maybe we can help you." (See Nehemiah 1–6.)

Again, the best way to prevent a man from accomplishing something is to get him to do a good thing—like have a meeting—instead of what he should be doing. Yet Nehemiah wasn't fooled. He told them, *"I am carrying on a great project and cannot go down. Why should the work stop while I leave it and go down to you?"* (Neh. 6:3).

REINFORCE YOUR PURPOSE

I can't emphasize strongly enough that knowing your purpose is crucial for your life's course. Every young person comes to a time when he or she leaves childhood and enters adulthood. That period is called adolescence. This is the time in which young people are trying to discover who they are and why they are. This is also often the time when we lose them or gain them—lose them to a destructive lifestyle and a wasted life or gain them for a positive, fulfilling future. Purpose, therefore, is key to a young person's effectiveness and happiness in life.

JESUS' PURPOSE WAS REINFORCED FROM HIS BIRTH.

Did Jesus have an adolescent problem? The answer is, very simply, no. Why? His purpose was reinforced from birth. His earthly mother and father were told why He was born. Somehow I believe that God would love for all parents to know Him so well that they would have an idea of the life purpose of their children.

The angel of the Lord said to Joseph, *"You are to give him the name Jesus, because he will save his people from their sins"* (Matt. 1:21). Joseph shared this message with Mary. When Jesus was born, Mary could talk to Him about His purpose. Even though, at the time, she didn't fully understand the implications of His name, she could tell Him, "You're going to be a Savior."

The Hebrew meaning of the name *Jesus* is "Jehovah-saved," or "the Lord is salvation." In essence, Jesus' name means "Savior." When He was a boy, His friends would say to Him, "Savior, come out and play with us." His parents would say to Him, "Savior, come in for supper." When people heard Him coming, they'd say, "Is that you, Jesus? How are you doing today, Savior?" All His life, He heard that

41

name. Yet it was not just a name; it was a reason for being, and He grew up with that purpose in His mind.

When Jesus was twelve years old, He went to Jerusalem with His parents to celebrate the Feast of the Passover. When the Feast was over, His parents started for home, thinking that Jesus was among the large group of relatives and friends traveling with them. When they didn't find Him, they went back to Jerusalem and finally found Him in the temple courts. They said, "Why did you leave us, Son? Why did you do this to us?" (See Luke 2:48.) His answer was very powerful. At twelve years of age, He was able to say to His parents, *"I must be about My Father's business"* (v. 49 NKJV).

How old are you?

Are you still questioning what you are about?

Are you still wondering what kind of business your Father is in and which part you are to play in the company?

Are you still "changing your major" in life every three years?

Do you find you can't graduate from God's preparatory school into God's work world?

Are you fifty years old and still looking for a job transfer?

I know it's not easy to take a hard look at yourself, but it's necessary if you're going to discover your true purpose in life.

You will be busy doing meaningful work when you learn why you are here. At twelve years of age, Jesus was busy with His purpose. Isn't that an exciting way to live? Don't give up on having a purposeful life, no matter what your age is. Get busy with the right thing.

PRINCIPLES FOR FINDING YOUR PURPOSE

How do you discover what's right? God has given us seven principles of purpose so that we can live successful, fulfilled lives. Write them on a sheet of paper and put them on your mirror so you can look at them every morning when you're getting ready for work. Use them as a book-mark in your Bible to remind yourself of them when you're praying and reading the Word. When you understand these principles, you'll be able to learn and live in your purpose:

1. God is a God of purpose.
2. God created everything with a purpose.
3. Not every purpose is known to us because we have lost our understanding of God's original intent for us.
4. Where purpose is not known, abuse is inevitable.
5. To discover the purpose of something, never ask the creation; ask the creator.
6. We find our purpose only in the mind of our Maker.
7. God's purpose is the key to our fulfillment.

1. GOD IS A GOD OF PURPOSE

God is a purposeful Being. He has a purpose for every-thing He has ever done. He established His purpose before He created what was needed to fulfill it. What He plans is intentional, meaningful, and guaranteed to succeed.

This theme is found throughout the Bible. Consider these Scriptures:

> *The LORD Almighty has sworn, "Surely, as I have planned, so it will be, and as I have purposed, so it will stand."* (Isa. 14:24)

> *The plans of the LORD stand firm forever, the purposes of his heart through all generations.* (Ps. 33:11)

> *As the rain and the snow come down from heaven, and do not return to it without watering the earth and making it bud and flourish, so that it yields seed for the sower and bread for the eater, so is my word that goes out from my mouth: It will not return to me empty, but will accomplish what I desire and achieve the purpose for which I sent it.* (Isa. 55:10–11)

Men swear by someone greater than themselves, and the oath confirms what is said and puts an end to all argument. Because God wanted to make the unchanging nature of his purpose very clear to the heirs of what was promised, he confirmed it with an oath.

(Heb. 6:16–17)

God has purposes that He determines beforehand and then carries out. These include plans for humanity as a whole and plans for males and females who carry out humanity's purposes. To bring this to a personal level, this includes plans for you and me. God does not do anything on a whim or without knowing the end result.

The origins of humanity are described in the book of Genesis, which means "beginning." However, the Creation that we read about in **GENESIS IS BOTH THE BEGINNING AND THE END RESULT.** Genesis was not the real beginning. I would like to call Genesis "the end result after God finished His thought processes." When God finished deciding what He wanted to do, then He created. First God predetermined, predestined, or purposed everything. Then He produced it.

This concept is crucial to our understanding of purpose. It means that Genesis was not the beginning of a supernatural experiment with an unknown outcome. Genesis was the beginning of the production of something that was sure. So, when we talk about what happened in Genesis, we're really talking about what happened after God finished thinking.

Therefore, in Genesis, we are looking at the start-up of the project, as I like to call it. Those of you who are studying project management know that this is an important step in the process of building. When you reach the start-up phase, it means that you have all the plans drawn, all the physical resources in place, all the management resources in order, and now you're ready to begin. That's Genesis.

Do you begin building a house when you dig the foundation? No, you begin building it when the idea is conceived.

This means that the finished house is in the unseen. People pass by the property, and they don't see it. However, to you who understand and know what is going to happen, it is already finished. Digging the foundation is the beginning of the implementation of your purpose. So, after you dig the foundation, when somebody asks you, "What are you doing?" your answer is very definite. You point to the architect's rendering of the house and say, "I am building this."

God revealed this truth to me in a very visual way. There is a street near where I live called Shirley Street. At one time, there was only a parking lot there. One day when I was driving along that street I saw a large sign with a beautifully painted picture of a building. There was no building on the site yet, but there was the big sign and the name of a building. It showed the landscape, the color of the building, the windows, everything. It was a detailed picture of what the completed building would look like. The sign said, "Coming soon."

I drove past the lot and sensed the Holy Spirit saying to me, "Did you see that?" I said, "See what?" He said, "Did you see the finish?" Did I see the finish? I drove by the post office and came back around to take another look at the painting. He said, "There it is. The finish." The construction company was showing us the end of their purpose. To have vision means to see something coming into view as if it were already there. The company had a vision for this building.

Likewise, God in His wisdom is not guessing about His plans for us—for humanity as a whole or for each of us individually. God has already decided on His purpose. He has the complete picture. It's on His drawing board. It's His vision for us. It isn't an afterthought. In Genesis 1, we read how He began to dig the foundation of humanity. We'll pick up on this theme in chapter 4, because it is essential to understanding the nature and purpose of the male.

What we need to understand at this point is that when God created the male and the female, He had already predetermined what they were supposed to be and do. They are not divine experiments. Together, they are an intentional divine project with a predetermined purpose.

2. GOD CREATED EVERYTHING WITH A PURPOSE

God created everything with a purpose in mind, and He also created it with the ability to fulfill its purpose. Everything God has made is the way it is because of why it was created. The *why* dictates its makeup. The purpose of a thing determines its nature, its design, and its features.

You don't make something until you know what you want and why you want it. You'll never find a manufacturer starting a project in a plant, hoping it will turn out to be something useful. Its purpose and design are complete before production starts. For example, if a manufacturer decides he wants to build an apparatus that can both record moving pictures onto a magnetic tape for replay and broadcast them live through the medium of television, then he has created a product, a video camera—but the manufacturer designed it first. What's more, everything in the video camera is necessary for its proper functioning. If you could look inside such a camera, you would see things that you didn't know were there and that you don't know the use for. Yet nothing in that product is there for the fun of it. As a matter of fact, because it is so expensive, there had better be nothing in it just for the fun of it.

THE PURPOSE OF SOMETHING DETERMINES ITS NATURE, DESIGN, AND FEATURES.

Let me give you another illustration that is even closer to home—your big toe. Are you aware that if your big toe were cut off, you would lose your balance and fall down? You probably never think about your big toe until you stub it. Then it just seems like an annoyance. Yet it keeps you standing up when you lean forward. Your big toe isn't there just for fun. Thank God for big toes! There's also a purpose for your fingernails. Some of you know exactly how important they are because you've had an accident and lost one. Your fingernails are there to protect the softer skin on your fingers.

Since God created everything with a purpose, both males and females need to go to Him if they want to know their true reason for being. If they try to change His plans or fight

against them, they are in essence fighting against themselves, because they're working against their own nature,
their own makeup, the way they function best based on the
Manufacturer's design. Moreover, because God is love, His
plans embody what is best for us, so they would also be
working against their own highest good.

God's purpose requires two genders working together in
cooperation to accomplish a mutual vision. Accordingly,
males and females have complementary designs that enable
them to fulfill God's purpose together.

3. NOT EVERY PURPOSE IS KNOWN TO US

Although everyone and everything on earth has a purpose, this does not mean that we are aware of their purposes. When human beings as a race turned their backs on
God and His ways, as we learn about in Genesis 3, they
ended up losing their knowledge of God's intent for themselves and for the world.

Rejecting God was the equivalent of buying a sophisti-
cated and intricate piece of equipment and then throwing
away the user's manual. If you get something to work under
those circumstances, it is only by pure chance. The more
likely scenario is that you will never get it to function properly. You will also miss out on the many features and functions it has to offer. It will never fulfill its complete purpose.

Likewise, humanity has not respected the fact that God's
creation and His directions for living were established for a
specific reason and that, if that purpose continues to be
abandoned, males and females will never function properly
as human beings. This is a very dangerous situation for
them to be in, because it leads right to the next principle.

4. WHERE PURPOSE IS NOT KNOWN, ABUSE IS INEVITABLE

Whenever purpose is not known, abuse is inevitable.
Suppose I'm Henry T. Ford. I'm going to add a motor to a
carriage and build a product called a motorcar. I know the
purpose before I build this vehicle. It will enable people to be
more mobile on land. Now suppose you decide, "I want to
use this motorcar as a boat," and you drive it off a cliff and
into the water. What will happen? You're probably going to
drown, and the car is going to be ruined. Why? The car was

built to fulfill a specific purpose, and if you do not use it according to its purpose, then you will likely be harmed in the process. We need to keep from driving off the cliff of life by understanding and fulfilling our purpose as human beings.

Here is another aspect of this principle: the penalty for drinking poison is death from poisoning. You don't need God to kill you after you have swallowed poison. What this means for us is that God doesn't have to do anything to judge us for abusing our lives. We judge ourselves by receiving the consequences of our participation in harmful practices based on our determination to live according to our own knowledge rather than His. Consequently, we are victims of our own decisions, not of God's judgment.

These examples demonstrate that if you don't know the purpose of something, you will misuse or abuse it in some way. That's why it's possible to be sincerely wrong. It's possible to be faithfully wrong. It's possible to be seriously wrong. You're serious, but you're wrong, because you don't know the purpose for the thing you're involved in. This principle holds true for everything, including people.

IF YOU'RE SINCERE, YET DON'T KNOW YOUR PURPOSE, YOU WILL BE SINCERELY WRONG.

How many people go into marriage very seriously? Most people do. They go to the church, stand at the altar, and say to their betrothed, "I will love you until I die." They're very serious. But then they "die" in three months. At least their love dies. Then their family and friends try to figure out what happened. Their marriage failed because they didn't understand the purpose of marriage, the purpose of a mate, or the purpose of family. Because they didn't understand these things, they abused their union.

People abuse things because they just don't know their purposes—or because they disregard those purposes. When males and females don't know God's intentions, they end up abusing each other, even if they don't mean to. If males are going to solve their current identity crisis and fulfill their purpose as men, husbands, and fathers, they must rediscover God's plan for them. Otherwise, they will hurt those around them, even if it's unintentional.

5. TO DISCOVER PURPOSE, NEVER ASK THE CREATION; ASK THE CREATOR

If you want to know the purpose of something, don't ask the thing itself. Why? It didn't plan, design, or build itself. Only the manufacturer knows the why and how of his product; no one else truly does. That is why he can claim perfect relationship with his product.

Therefore, if you're going to use something, the first question you need to ask is, "Who made this?" If you buy a certain kind of guitar, you need to consult the manufacturer who made that particular guitar. That is why the company includes an instructional booklet with the instrument; the booklet tells you how to use the guitar based on its purpose. You don't use it to paddle a boat. You don't use it to play baseball. In other words, the manufacturer sent you the manual to protect you from abusing the product and so you could have the full enjoyment of it.

The point is this: *to understand how we function as human beings—as males and females—we need to go to the Manual given to us by the Designer and Manufacturer who created us: the Bible.* God knew exactly what He wanted when He thought of the male. Remember that He created both male and female after He had decided what each should be in order to fulfill His purposes and plans, and that He designed them accordingly.

This means that He is the only One who knows how humanity is intended to function. If you have any questions about why you are here, you should check the Manual. If you don't know the purpose of a thing, all you can do is experiment. Everybody who doesn't know his or her purpose is just experimenting with life.

Let me use marriage as an illustration again. Do you know what most marriages are today? Big experiments. "I don't really know what a wife is for, but I'm old enough to get married, so I'm going to have one." You get married because you're twenty-five. All right, then what? Do you know what you have? "No, but she looks good." What's a wife for? "Hey, man, to have sex with and to clean the kitchen." This is a big experiment. But guess what? After three weeks, you realize she doesn't agree with your definition. The experiment isn't working. She isn't cleaning those dishes, and she isn't into being a living sacrifice every night. She begins to ask for things like time. She wants love and affection and attention. She wants appreciation. "Hey, I didn't bargain for all that." Well, my friend, marriage is not a trial run.

LIFE IS NOT A TRIAL RUN.

Again, whenever you don't know the purpose of a thing, you're experimenting. That's what many people—especially young people—are doing with life. They don't know what education is for, so they treat school like an experiment. They skip classes and spend their time partying, then they flunk out. They experiment with sex and sexual identity, and they end up with all kinds of problems. They experiment with drugs and hurt their bodies.

When I was a boy, I was tempted to experiment in order to find out about life. I'm grateful God protected me from much of that. But many of the young people whom I grew up with did not make it through their experimentation. The experiment blew up. Some are dead. The bodies of others are contaminated and wrecked from using destructive substances. They didn't know the purpose of the elements they were using.

I'd like to say to the young people reading this book: if you want to know why you were born, the worst people to ask are your friends, because your friends are trying to figure out why they're here, too. If you want to know your reason for existence, don't ask another product; ask the Manufacturer. Everyone else is guessing.

What we've been doing all these years is asking the product why it exists. Because the world doesn't understand much about the reason for the existence of things, it functions like one big experimental lab. All of us seem to have been assuming the position of scientists. We have imagined that we have the time and intelligence to discover the reason for our existence through experimentation. Then we find out that life is short, and that we're very poor researchers.

Life is too precious to treat like a trial run. The only way to avoid the cost of trial and error is to learn the purpose of your life. Think about a car mechanic. If he's just experimenting, he won't last long in the automotive business. If he says, "I wonder what this part is for? Let me guess what section of the engine I should attach it to," that's experimentation. He doesn't know what the manufacturer had in mind.

Well, if you wouldn't let an inexperienced mechanic work on your car, what about your life? No university professor knows people well enough to write a definitive book about what makes us tick. No psychologist or psychiatrist truly knows me. God wrote a book on His product, and the product is me. Tell yourself, "I'm an expensive product. I won't let anyone experiment with me." It's a dangerous thing for us to experiment with this precious commodity called life.

Therefore, if a man wants to know his reason for living, He must look to God and His Manual—not to other males. If he looks to himself or others, he will travel an unreliable and hazardous course in life.

6. WE FIND PURPOSE ONLY IN THE MIND OF OUR MAKER

If you remember this principle all your life, you'll be safe: before you buy something, check to see who made it. Right away, you'll know what was in the mind of the maker. If you buy a shirt on sale at a discount store, and you see the store's label in the collar, you'll treat it differently than if you buy a Pierre Cardin shirt. You might toss the discount shirt on a chair, but you'll put the designer shirt on a hanger in your closet.

We need to understand the mind of our Maker. How do we do this? By learning how He thinks. The only way for us to succeed is by discovering and living in the purposes of our Maker, by undergoing a transformation in the way we think about ourselves based on His original intentions for us. That transformation comes about by a renewal of our minds:

Therefore, I urge you, brothers, in view of God's mercy, to offer your bodies as living sacrifices, holy and pleasing to God—this is your spiritual act of worship. Do not conform any longer to the pattern of this world, but be transformed by the renewing of your mind. Then you will be able to test and approve what God's will is—his good, pleasing and perfect will. (Rom. 12:1–2)

God's ways will transform your spirit, your mind, and your outlook. When you present yourself to God and learn from Him, you will begin to understand His purpose. *"The law of the LORD is perfect, reviving the soul. The statutes of the LORD are trustworthy, making wise the simple"* (Ps. 19:7).

The greatest way for you to find purpose is to yield your life to the Manufacturer. You shouldn't come to God because it's the religious thing to do. You shouldn't come to God because "everybody" is doing it. You shouldn't come to God because it's good to be a part of the church. You should come to God because you want to find out how not to waste your life. No one knows you like the One who made you. That's the bottom line.

We are so special to God that He sent His only Son to die for us. There must be something unique about each one of us for God to want us to receive salvation so that we can fulfill the purpose for which He gave us life. We need to seek Him earnestly in order to discover that purpose. *"You will seek me and find me when you seek me with all your heart"* (Jer. 29:13).

Thus, the male will fulfill his purpose only if he seeks the mind of his Maker with all his heart. When God's plans unfold before him, his fragmented life will become an orderly whole, and he can become the man he was meant to be.

7. GOD'S PURPOSE IS THE KEY TO OUR FULFILLMENT

You can never be totally and completely satisfied until you find your purpose and then live in it. You cannot *do* what you're supposed to do until you *discover* what you are supposed to do. And if you do what you're not supposed to do, you're not going to be fulfilled. You're wasting time. You're abusing your life. Stop it right now.

I was speaking about purpose at a church in Baton Rouge, Louisiana. A lady came up to me after the service and said, "I'm fifty-six years old, brother. Where were you fifty-six years ago?" I said, "What do you mean?" She said, "You're the first person ever to come into my life and help me understand that I have a reason for living—and I can't give an account of fifty-six years right now. Where were you for fifty-six years?"

Sometimes people begin to feel the way that woman did; they're distressed because they've wasted so much time. If this is your situation, don't be discouraged. One of the wonderful things about God is that He has a way of restoring the years that the locusts have eaten. (See Joel 2:23–26.) When you go to Him, He knows how to make up for the time that you've lost.

Yet God would prefer that we follow Him and know our purpose all our lives. That is why the Word of God says very strongly to young people, *"Remember your Creator in the days of your youth"* (Eccl. 12:1). The Bible is saying to us, "Remember God now—not when you've finished partying and ruining your health with drugs, alcohol, and tobacco, so that you say, 'Well, I'm sick now; I'd better go find God.'" Don't wait until after you have messed up your life to remember God.

GOD KNOWS HOW TO MAKE UP FOR THE TIME YOU HAVE LOST.

"Remember your Creator in the days of your youth." Why? God wants you to remember the Manufacturer early so that He can set you on course for your entire life.

God didn't say, "Remember the university." He didn't say, "Remember the school guidance counselor," or "Remember what your friends are saying." They can give you only their opinions about what you should do. God said, "Remember your Creator, the Manufacturer, the One who made you. Remember Him first while you're young." Why? So that the evil days won't rob your life.

Some of you know what I'm talking about because you've been there and now regret it. Some of you might still be in the middle of it. Others of you might not be using harmful substances, but you're still ruining your life. You're working fourteen hours a day trying to be "successful," but you're not doing what you were put on the earth to do. You're not going to be fulfilled.

Wouldn't it be great to live every day effectively, doing exactly what you were born to do? There's no fulfillment without knowing your purpose.

Remember the painting of that building on Shirley Street? After I had driven past the sign the second time, the **DO YOU KNOW WHERE YOU'RE HEADED?** Holy Spirit said to me, "If you were to see the men working on that project, digging up all the mud and muck, all the rocks and everything, making big holes, and if you were to ask them what they were doing, they would say, 'We're moving toward that. We are building that.' They could tell you exactly where they were headed." I have never forgotten that lesson.

I have a question for you: is your life similar to that? If someone were to ask you what you're doing, could you tell them you're headed somewhere? Could you tell them where? Are you so clear about your dream that you could paint a picture of it?

If you know where you're going, then when someone doesn't understand the reason for the mud, the muck, the water, and the hole, it doesn't matter. All that might not look right, but you see, that's the process. The process gets really messy sometimes. When you're in the midst of the process, your life might not look like it's becoming anything. But take careful note: there's a painting of you. God has painted it for you in His Word. Anytime you get bogged down in the mud and the muck, every time you get discouraged, you can look at that painting.

When a person works in construction, sometimes the contractor will tell him just to dig a trench. He can't see what this trench has to do with anything, but he has to trust him. He digs the trench because he knows the contractor sees things he doesn't know about. Likewise, God is in the business of constructing us and our lives. He is the Contractor. Sometimes He will tell you to do something, and He won't explain much about it.

You may be in the middle of something right now that He's told you to do, but that you don't understand; it doesn't seem to make any sense. You feel like you're just digging a trench. You're saying, "This isn't what I bargained for." Maybe your job is a trench. Maybe your marriage is a trench. But when you are pursuing God and His purposes, He's saying, "Don't quit. You don't understand. Just stay where you are. We're building something here. Just dig the trench."

A man may be able to see the outcome of God's purposes in his life twenty years into the future or only one day ahead. Yet if he is living in God's plans for him, he has found the key to his existence.

GOD PUT YOUR PURPOSE WITHIN YOU

Becoming what God has purposed for you not only allows you to live effectively, but also to worship your Creator, who has given you ideas, talents, resources, and energy to fulfill His desires and plans for your life. Proverbs 20:5 says, *"The purposes of a man's heart are deep waters, but a man of understanding draws them out."* That's a powerful statement, isn't it? *"The purposes of a man's heart are deep waters."* That means your purpose is inside you. God has placed it deeply within you. However, in order to draw it out, you need to be assisted by God's wisdom and revelation—because your purpose was born in the mind of your Maker.

Remember that God created the male with a specific purpose in mind, and He designed him uniquely for that purpose. Therefore, a man possesses inherent characteristics and qualities that are necessary for his functioning and fulfillment as a male. Moreover, when a man identifies, understands, effectively applies, and manifests these qualities in his life and relationships, the female will also experience a fulfillment she has always longed for.

As we've seen, it is beneficial to look at the overall picture before seeing how all the details fit into it. In order for a man to know God's purpose for him as a male and as an individual, he first needs to see God's purposes for humanity as a whole. In the next chapter, we are going to take a close look at God's wisdom and revelation in regard to the creation of man.

PRINCIPLES

1. God is a God of purpose.

2. What God plans is intentional, meaningful, and guaranteed to succeed.

3. God created everything with a purpose.

4. The purpose of something determines its nature, design, and features.

5. Not every purpose is known to us because we have lost our understanding of God's original intent for us.

6. Where purpose is not known, abuse is inevitable.

7. To discover the purpose of something, never ask the creation; ask the creator.

8. If we don't know the purpose for our lives, we're just experimenting.

9. When you go to God, He knows how to make up for the time that you lost from not knowing your purpose.

10. We find our purpose only in the mind of our Maker.

11. God's purpose is the key to our fulfillment.

12. God put your purpose within you. To draw it out, you need to be assisted by His wisdom and revelation.

3

THE CREATION OF MAN

Men can know the true meaning of their existence only by understanding who they are in relation to God's creation of mankind as a whole. They need to see how they fit into God's great picture of humanity, which He designed and then constructed when the world began.

The first thing we must realize is that there is a distinction between being *man* and being *male,* and that each has unique purposes for being. What do I mean by this? The account of Creation in the first two chapters of Genesis reveals the essential difference. Genesis 1 is a declaration chapter. It declares what God did in Creation. Genesis 2 is an explanation chapter. It explains how God accomplished His act of Creation and shows how the creation of man relates to the creation of man's two physical manifestations: male and female.

In Genesis 1:26–28, we read,

> *Then God said, "Let us make man in our image, in our likeness, and let them rule ["have dominion" NKJV] over the fish of the sea and the birds of the air, over the livestock, over all the earth, and over all the creatures that move along the ground." So God created man in his own image, in the image of God he created him; male and female he created them. God blessed them and said to them, "Be fruitful and increase in number; fill the earth and subdue it."*

CREATED IN GOD'S IMAGE

The first thing we learn from this passage is that man was made in the image of God. When God made man, He essentially drew man out of Himself, so that the essence of man would be just like Him. Since *"God is spirit"* (John 4:24), He created man as spirit. Spirit is eternal. Man was created as an eternal being, because God is eternal.

It is important to recognize that we are not yet talking about male and female. It was mankind that God created in His image. Man is spirit, and spirits have no gender. The Bible never talks about a male or female spirit.

What was the reason God created mankind in His image? He didn't create any of the animals or plants in His image. He didn't even make angels in His image. Man is the only being of God's creation that is like Him.

TO BE HIS OFFSPRING

God created mankind for relationship with Himself—to be His family, His offspring, spiritual children of God. The nature of God is to love and to give. Since *"God is love"* (1 John 4:8, 16), He wanted a being who could be the object of His love and grace. He wanted man to be the recipient of all that He is and all that He has.

The fact that man was created in God's image is an awesome revelation about our relationship to Him. God desired children who would be like Himself. **GOD IS SPIRIT, AND SO HE CREATED MAN AS A SPIRIT.** Yet He didn't just desire it, then walk away without doing anything about it. He conceived His desire and made it a reality. He became "pregnant" with what He was desiring. Once God conceived, He began to prepare for the "birth" or creation of man. Before there was anything at all on the earth, there was God, and God was pregnant with us.

What do we call a woman who is pregnant? Expectant. God was in expectation of man's birth, so right away He began to prepare a "nursery" for His children, even before there was any physical evidence of His offspring. God's desire for His children caused Him to create the universe in preparation for their arrival.

Let me tell you what we've been taught, and it's not biblical. We've been taught that God created the universe, and *then* He decided to make man. That's not the way it happened. God first decided to make man, and that was the reason for the creation of the world.

When my wife and I were expecting our first child, we had the nursery fixed up before the baby arrived. I remember the day it was finished and we stood looking at the whole thing. We had thoroughly cleaned the room. We had the new crib, pillow, sheets, powder, baby oil, diapers, baby food, and everything else all ready. We had little pictures on the walls. There was no baby, but everything the baby would need and use was ready. Then we stepped back, looked at the room, and said, "This is good." What were we doing? Preparing. That's exactly what God was doing in Genesis 1 when He made the world in preparation for the creation of man.

Just as a new baby is at the center of his parents' thoughts, mankind was and is at the center of God's thoughts. The wonder of this idea struck King David one day. He said, *"When I consider your heavens, the work of your fingers, the moon and the stars, which you have set in place, what is man that you are mindful of him, the son of man that you care for him?"* (Ps. 8:3–4). David asked God, in effect, "Why are you thinking only about us?" Although the psalm doesn't give us God's answer, I think His reply would be, "Every time you see the moon and the stars, and everything else I've created, I want you to know that all that exists because of you."

We are so important to God that He created the entire universe for us. Not only that, He created it with great care to make sure we had the best environment in which to live. Everything God created keeps everything else in balance. For example, when He made our solar system, He created the sun to be a light for us, and then He carefully placed the planets around it. I can imagine God making adjustments so that the solar system would be just right for us. I see Him pushing the earth out a bit, then saying, "No, it's too close to the sun. That's too hot. Let's pull it back a little. Now it's too cold. They'll freeze. Ah, this is just right. The conditions are perfect. The baby will do fine." Then I imagine Him saying, "Children like colors, so let's cause some vivid flowers to spring up from the ground. That's a beau-

MAN IS THE REASON FOR THE UNIVERSE.

tiful rose; they'll like that. Let's put some colors on the fish, too. Now, we've already created the sunset, but let's make the ozone layer run right past the light so that it changes color. Let the light come through the atmosphere and the stratosphere, so that when it hits them it will turn purple, yellow, blue, and pink." I see Him thinking about man's future physical needs. "Now we must have a lot of food for the baby. We'll need some fruits and vegetables. We also need to separate the salt water from the fresh, so that the baby can drink. Now—everything is in order. The nursery is ready!"

I submit to you that man is the reason for the universe. I didn't say man is the center of it. Humanists say that man is the center of the universe. That is wrong. God is the center of everything. He "[upholds] *all things by the word of his power*" (Heb. 1:3 KJV). It is He who is the center of life. Everything He created and every movement of our being exists in Him. Yet because we are His offspring, He created the universe just for us.

When God finished creating the world, He called everything good. (See Genesis 1:4–25.) I believe He said this because everything was ready. It was after God called the physical world good that He said, *"Let us make man"* (v. 26). What's so interesting about this is that the heavens and the earth were created first because of their purpose. Some people might say, "Well, if the heavens and earth were created first, does that mean that they are more important than man?" No. They were just leading up to the advent of man. Their purpose was to be a perfect environment for God's children. When my wife and I were getting the nursery ready, we had the crib, powder, and all the other material things in the room first. Did that mean they were more important than the baby? No. Those things were there only because of the baby. The same is true concerning man's relationship to the physical world. Ephesians 1:4 explains the order of priority in this way: *"For he chose us in him **before** the creation of the world"* (emphasis added).

TO HAVE FELLOWSHIP WITH HIM

Another reason man was created in God's image was to have fellowship with Him, like a close family relationship. The only reason man can have this fellowship with God is that God made man to be spirit, just as He is Spirit. *"God is spirit, and his worshipers must worship in spirit and in truth"* (John 4:24).

Although God is the Creator, He has always emphasized that He is man's Father. It wasn't His desire to be primarily thought of by man as an awesome God or a *"consuming fire"* (Deut. 4:24). Although at times it is difficult for our religious minds to grasp this concept, God wants us to approach Him as a child would a loving father.

God and humanity were made for one another. That is why, no matter how many relationships you have or how many gifts you buy for others, in the end, you aren't going to be satisfied until you love God. God must have the primary place in your life. Your love was designed to be fulfilled in Him.

TO MANIFEST HIS NATURE

God created man in His image so that man could also reflect His character and personality. When God created man, heaven and earth stood in awe of this amazing being who manifested the Creator's very nature and reflected His glory.

Consider this remarkable verse in Psalm 82: *"I said, 'You are gods, and all of you are children of the Most High'"* (v. 6 NKJV). This verse is speaking of mankind. It calls us "gods" and "children of the Most High." Why are we called little gods? It is because as children of the Most High God, we have His nature and share His purposes. Physically, we are children of men, but spiritually, we are children of God.

Two foundational aspects of God's character are love and light, and man is meant to exhibit these qualities. However, man's being made in God's image does not mean that man can reveal these qualities apart from Him. Man was always meant to reveal God's nature in the context of being continually connected to Him in fellowship. First John 4:16 says, *"Whoever lives in love lives in God, and God in him,"* and Proverbs 20:27 says, *"The spirit of man is the candle of the LORD"* (KJV). This means that when you have fellowship with God, you reflect His light. You show the nature of God, for *"God is light; in him there is no darkness at all"* (1 John 1:5).

PHYSICALLY, WE ARE CHILDREN OF MEN, BUT SPIRITUALLY, WE ARE CHILDREN OF GOD.

God also created man to demonstrate His wisdom and the goodness of His precepts. This purpose is part of God's eternal plans, and it culminated in the coming of Christ Jesus and the birth of the church:

> *His intent was that now, through the church, the manifold wisdom of God should be made known to the rulers and authorities in the heavenly realms, according to his eternal purpose which he accomplished in Christ Jesus our Lord.* (Eph. 3:10–11)

TO SHARE HIS RULE

God said, *"Let us make man in our image, in our likeness, and **let them rule** ["have dominion" NKJV]"* (Gen. 1:26, emphasis added). Man was created to share God's authority. God never wanted to rule by Himself. Love doesn't think in those terms. You can always tell a person who is full of love. He doesn't want to do anything for his purposes alone. A selfish person wants all the glory, all the credit, all the recognition, all the attention, all the power, all the authority, all the rights, and all the privileges. But a person of love wants others to share in what he has.

Note that the word *"man"* in Genesis 1:26 refers to the spirit-being created in God's image. The purpose of dominion was given to man the spirit. This was before the creation of male and female, which we will discuss in more detail shortly. Therefore, spiritually, both male and female have the same responsibility toward the earth because rule was given to the spirit-man, which resides in both of them.

The account of Creation reveals an interesting fact that we often overlook today. God didn't create man for heaven. He created man for the earth. God is the Ruler of heaven, and He made man to express His authority on earth. He said, "I want what's happening in heaven to happen in the created world; I want My rule to extend to another realm, but I don't want to do it directly. I want man to share My rule." The plan of Creation was this: as God ruled the unseen realm in heaven, man would rule the visible realm on earth, with God and man enjoying continual communion through their spiritual natures. God said to man, in essence, "Let Me rule through you so you can appreciate, enjoy, and share in rulership and know how it feels to be 'little gods.'"

GOD DIDN'T CREATE MAN FOR HEAVEN. HE CREATED MAN FOR THE EARTH.

It's important to realize that man was created not only for fellowship with God but also with a responsibility to carry out. I want to emphasize this point because sometimes people use their worship of God as an excuse for negligence in other areas of their lives. They say, "I was created only to love the Lord, worship the Lord, and praise the Lord." These things are good and necessary. However, you can't spend all your time in the sanctuary worshiping, praising, and singing. There comes a time when you have to carry out your responsibility to demonstrate what your relationship with the Lord means in terms of living and ruling in the world.

Man has been given the freedom to exhibit creativity while governing the physical earth and all the other living things that dwell in it. The earth is to be ruled over, taken care of, fashioned, and molded by beings made in the image of their Creator. In this way, man is meant to reflect the loving and creative Spirit of God.

TO EXPAND THE FAMILY BUSINESS

We also need to understand that when God created man to share His authority, it was in the context of man's relationship to Him as His offspring. God didn't create man to be a servant but to be a son who is involved in running the family business. This was His plan for mankind from the beginning. He has always wanted His children to help Him fulfill His purposes.

This means that God doesn't want man to work *for* Him; He wants man to work *with* Him. The Bible says that we are *"God's fellow workers"* (2 Cor. 6:1) or *"workers together with him"* (KJV). In the original Greek, *"fellow workers"* means those who "cooperate," who "help with," who "work together."

It's common to hear people say, "I'm working for Jesus." If you are working *for* Jesus, you are still a hired hand. When you understand the family business, then you become a worker alongside Christ.

TO RELY ON THE FATHER FOR PERSONAL NEEDS

What are some of the implications of our being God's children, working in His business? First, we don't have to worry about our day-to-day living expenses. If your father and mother owned a prosperous business, and they put you in the business to run it, should you wonder where you will get food to eat? Should you wonder where you will get water to drink? Should you wonder where you're going to get clothes to wear? No, you are family, and you are going to be provided for.

If you are hired to work in the business only as an employee, then you don't know the company's true financial condition. In addition, if you want more money, you have to ask for a raise. You have to work hard to receive a bonus. You have to impress the boss so that you can get just a little increase in salary. You may also live in fear of being fired. However, if you are a son, you know just how well the company is doing.

In God's company, there's always plenty of provision to go around, and you can rely on that with confidence. Jesus said,

> *Do not worry, saying, "What shall we eat?" or "What shall we drink?" or "What shall we wear?" For the pagans run after all these things, and your heavenly Father knows that you need them. But seek first his kingdom and his righteousness, and all these things will be given to you as well.* (Matt. 6:31–33)

Jesus didn't say, "The boss knows that you need these things." He said, "Your *Father* knows that you need these things." We can trust our Father, the wealthy Businessman, to provide for all our needs.

TO RELY ON THE FATHER FOR KINGDOM NEEDS

When Jesus knew that His earthly ministry was about to end and that He would be crucified, resurrected, and then return to His heavenly Father, He talked to His disciples about their role in advancing the family business on earth. *"I no longer call you servants, because a servant does not know his master's business. Instead, I have called you friends, for everything that I learned from my Father I have made known to you"* (John 15:15). What was Jesus' reason for calling His disciples His friends? He said, in effect, "The servant doesn't know what the boss is doing. I call you friends because I have told you everything the Father has revealed to Me."

IN GOD'S COMPANY, THERE'S ALWAYS PLENTY OF PROVISION TO GO AROUND.

Think about how large and prosperous God's business is. It is so big that God says He can supply all your needs

(Phil. 4:19). I don't think that in this context He is referring to your smaller needs, such as a house, a car, clothes, or food. Remember that He told us we don't even have to ask for those things. Therefore, He must be talking about leads for further investment for the purpose of expanding the company business. He is saying, in essence, "The company has so much collateral that My children never have to worry about materials for further investment."

GOD DESIRES TO EXTEND HIS RULE FROM THE UNSEEN TO THE SEEN.

I believe that if we will get busy spreading the company's influence and building its interests, our access to resources will be unclogged. (See Matthew 6:33.) God created man to be His offspring and to work in His business, and He has all the resources we need to fulfill this purpose.

TO EXECUTE HIS RIGHTEOUS JUDGMENT

Man was created in God's image for yet another reason: to execute His righteous judgment. In all the prophecies about the Messiah, especially in Isaiah, Jeremiah, and Daniel, you will find that this was also the main purpose for Christ's coming to earth. It was the result of His life, ministry, death, and resurrection. All these things were connected to His fulfilling His purpose of executing righteous judgment on the earth.

The reason this is also the purpose of man is that it is God's intention that we rule the earth through the Spirit of Christ. Recall that, through man, God desires to extend His rule from the unseen to the seen. He wants to expose His character, nature, principles, precepts, and righteous judgment to the visible world. Even though the fall of man brought humanity out from under God's purposes, Christ redeemed us so we could be restored to His original plans for us. Dominion over the earth, including exercising righteous judgment, is not a temporary but an eternal assignment from God to man.

Because of the Fall, when we die, our spirits will separate from our bodies, and we will go to be with God in heaven. Again, it was never God's intention that man would work in heaven. Even though in our spiritual growth and development we will learn to have dominion over spiritual as well as physical things (see 1 Corinthians 6:3), God gave man the earth to rule. Since God's purposes never change, He made provision in His plan of redemption for man to fulfill that purpose.

God made us a promise. He said that when we come to the head office (heaven), we will stay there only for a while. There will come a Day when our bodies will be resurrected and rejoined with our spirits, so that He can send us back to finish the job. (See 1 Corinthians 15:42–44, 52–53; Isaiah 65:17.)

If you are finding it hard to take all this in, read the book of Revelation. God keeps on talking about thrones, reigning with Him, and ruling with Him. The reason we will reign is that Jesus came to bring righteous judgment back to the earth. He came to bring it back to where it was supposed to be in the first place. That has always been God's purpose for man. God made you a manager, and He always fulfills His eternal purposes.

He isn't going to raise you from the dead just to live with Him forever. He's going to raise you from the dead so that you can get on with your work. That's why the Scripture says that when Jesus returns to earth and we are resurrected, we will reign with Him (Rev. 5:10). *Reign* means what? To have dominion, to administrate.

CREATED MALE AND FEMALE

Therefore, God created man so that He could have someone to love, someone who would work with Him in His purposes for the earth. Yet the earth is a physical entity, and man is spirit. The earth needed someone with a physical body to live in it and take care of it. God knew this would be necessary, and that is a primary reason He created the male and the female.

"So God created man in his own image, in the image of God he created him; male and female he created them" (Gen. 1:27). After God created man, He

AFTER GOD CREATED MAN, HE PLACED HIM IN TWO PHYSICAL "HOUSES": MALE AND FEMALE.

placed him in two physical "houses": male and female. This means that man the spirit exists within every male and every female. All of us—males and females alike—are man. The essence of both male and female is the resident spirit within them, called "man." Genesis 5:1–2 says, *"When God created man, he made him in the likeness of God. He created them male and female and blessed them. And when they were created, he called them* [together] *'man.'"*

Why did God take man, who is spirit, and put him in two separate physical entities rather than just one? It was because He wanted man to fulfill two distinct purposes. We'll explore the significance of this fact in more detail in coming chapters. For now, we need to remember that the spirit-man has no gender and that, in order to fulfill His eternal purposes, God used two physical forms to express the spiritual being made in His image.

Therefore, whether you are male or female, the person who lives inside you—the essential you—is the spirit-man. Although males and females have differences, they are of the same essence.

Since human beings fellowship with God and worship Him through their spirits, this means that men and women both have direct spiritual access to God and are individually responsible to Him.

"CREATED" VERSUS "MADE"

Genesis 1:26–27 implies that the process through which God created man was different from the process through which He produced the male and female. We can think of the distinction in this way: God *created* man, but He *made* male and female. The words for *"made"* in verse

26 and *"created"* in verse 27 are different words in the Hebrew. *"Make"* comes from *asah,* which means to form out of something that is already there. *"Created"* comes from *bara,* which means to form out of nothing. These verses say that God *created* man in His own image, but that God also *made* man. God used both of these words in reference to how He brought man into existence. In effect, He was saying, "I will both create him and make him. I will create him out of nothing and I will make him out of something."

Recall that God created the spirit-man out of His own being rather than out of anything from the physical world. Man was not created from matter; man came out of God's Spirit. Therefore, the part of man that was made from "nothing" came out of God. God spoke him into existence, similar to the way in which He spoke, *"'Let there be light,' and there was light"* (Gen. 1:3). Yet when God made male and female, He used material from the physical world that He had already created.

GOD CREATED MAN, BUT HE MADE MALE AND FEMALE.

Recognizing this distinction is critical to understanding our purpose in the world as both spiritual beings made in God's image and physical beings who carry out man's God-ordained purposes in the world. It is also essential to the male's understanding of who he is and how he is meant to relate to the female. We will see the practical implications of these purposes in the next chapter.

PRINCIPLES

1. Men can know the true meaning of their existence only by understanding who they are in relation to God's creation of mankind as a whole.

2. There is a distinction between being *man* and being *male.*

3. Mankind was created in the image of God.

4. God created man to be spirit, as He is Spirit.

5. Man was created to be God's offspring, to have fellowship with Him, to manifest His nature, to share His rule, to expand the family business, to rely on the Father for personal needs and for kingdom needs, and to execute God's righteous judgment.

6. After God created man, He placed him in two physical "houses": male and female.

7. Man—the spirit-man—resides within both male and female.

8. God *created* man, but He *made* male and female.

9. God made male and female because He wanted man to fulfill two distinct purposes on the physical earth.

4

GOD'S PURPOSE FOR
THE MALE

GOD DESIGNED AND EQUIPPED THE MALE TO CARRY OUT
EVERY PURPOSE AND FUNCTION HE HAS BEEN GIVEN.

Many men are still wondering why they exist. Yet the Creator of man did not leave us guessing about who the male is supposed to be and what he is designed to do. In this chapter, we are going to explore God's original intentions for men, so that there's no more worry, no more guessing as to their reason for being. We turn again to Proverbs 19:21 for the vital truth, *"Many are the plans in a man's heart, but it is the Lord's purpose that prevails."* Many are our opinions of what man should be, but the Lord's purpose is the only one that counts—and this purpose is the key to our fulfillment.

What we will be looking at is the male's ideal purpose. This is not where we are right now. Yet God's ideal is what we should be moving toward; and by His grace, we will.

THE CREATION OF THE MALE-MAN

We first need to remember that God creates according to the requirements of His purposes. In the previous chapter, we learned that God desired to dominate and influence the planet through mankind, and so He created man—the spirit—in His image and then placed the man in two physical "houses," male and female. *"So God created man in his own image, in the image of God he created him; male and female he created them"* (Gen. 1:27).

I would like to point out here that since the spirit-man dwells in both male and female, we may refer to the male as

71

a "male-man" and to the female as a "female-man." This will remind us that men and women are both "man." The distinctions between men and women are physical and functional, rather than of their essence.

The purpose of man—the spirit—and the purpose of the male are two different things, although they are related. Man was created in God's image for the purposes we discussed in the previous chapter. Male was made to serve the needs of man on earth and to enable him to fulfill his purpose.

Genesis 2 gives us a more detailed explanation of the manner in which God made male and female. First, He **THE MALE WAS MADE TO SERVE THE NEEDS OF MAN ON EARTH.** *"formed"* the male: *"The LORD God formed the man from the dust of the ground and breathed into his nostrils the breath of life, and the man became a living being"* (Gen. 2:7). The male was made first, and there was an interlude of time before the female was made. There is much we can learn about God's purposes for the male by what the male saw, heard, and learned during this interlude.

Remember that the purpose of something determines its nature, its design, and its features. This means that the nature, design, and qualities of males were decided upon by God and created by Him according to what He determined was best for the sake of His purposes.

ELEMENTS OF THE MALE'S PURPOSE

The purpose of the male may be summed up as *his priority, his position,* and *his assignment.*

- *Priority* refers to the man's order in creation and what this means in regard to his reason for being.

- *Position* refers to the environment and place in which the man is to carry out his purpose.

- *Assignment* means the functions or tasks that the man has been given.

1. THE MALE'S PRIORITY

The order in which the male was created gives us the first indication of his reason for being. Why did God make the male first? It was not because the male was better, but because of his purpose.

When you think about it, God really made only one human being. When He created the female, He didn't go back to the soil, but He fashioned her from the side of the man. (See Genesis 2:21–23.) Only the male came directly from the earth. This was because the male was designed by God to be the foundation of the human family. The woman came out of the man rather than the earth because she was designed to rest on the man—to have the male as her support.

THE MALE IS THE FOUNDATION OF THE HUMAN FAMILY.

I believe that the foundation of society, the infrastructure God intended for this world, has been misunderstood. We often say that the family is the foundation of society. It is very true that the family is the adhesive that holds it together. Yet God did not start to build earthly society with a family. He began it with one person. He began it with the male-man.

Remember our discussion of the principles of purpose in chapter 2? Because God is a God of purpose, He planned everything before He began to create, so that when He started digging the foundation, He knew exactly what He wanted and what the completed picture would look like. But he had to start with the foundation.

Have you ever seen a contractor build a house starting with the roof? Have you ever seen a guy walk into an empty lot and hold up a window in the air, trying to get it to stay? You don't start with the windows. You don't start with the roof. You don't start with the rafters. Likewise, God starts like any other builder. The priority in building is always what you need to do first. You start with the foundation.

God's communications to man in the Bible indicate the importance He places on building from the foundation up.

What did Jesus describe as our foremost priority? What we're building on. (See Matthew 7:24–27.) He said, in effect, "Now, some of you are building on sand. Your building looks good, but I don't care how good your building looks. If your foundation isn't right, there's going to be a great crash."

Paul said, *"No one can lay any* [spiritual] *foundation other than the one already laid"* (1 Cor. 3:11). What—or rather, who—is that foundation? *"Jesus Christ"* (v. 11). So God does not think of foundations in terms of only concrete and water, but also in terms of people.

That is why, when God began to build the human race, He began by laying the foundation of the male. God placed males at the bottom of the entire building of humanity. This means that society is only as strong as its males. If the males don't learn what it means to be a strong foundation in God, then society is sunk. That goes for America, Canada, Russia, China—all the nations of the world. If the male leaves the home, or if he neglects his responsibility, you have a house built on sand. It becomes very difficult for those windows to stay intact. The rafters rock when the pressures come because the man isn't there.

WHEN MEN HAVE CRACKS IN THE SUBSTRUCTURE OF THEIR LIVES, THE WHOLE BUILDING OF HUMANITY IS ON SHAKY GROUND.

You children of divorce know what I'm talking about. Your mother was a single parent and had to struggle, so that you weren't sure what was going to happen to the family. Of course, you are grateful to your mother. You really appreciate what she did, and you thank God that she weathered the storm and got through life. She did well. However, you all suffered the trauma of a missing foundation.

When the male-man has cracks and faults in the substructure of his life, then the whole building is on shaky ground. Now men, let's talk. This is the year you must decide to get yourself on solid ground, for as the man goes, so goes the family, society, and the world. Take a look at the condition of our societies and nations. How do you think the men are doing?

Our societies are in a mess because, as the foundation, men have become sandy—uncertain and unstable. How can you build a human race on a foundation that is full of sand mixed with straw? A foundation is always measured by how much weight can be placed on it.

When I was building my house, the architect and contractor were discussing all these figures, and I got confused. I was sitting there acting as if I knew what they were talking about. They were saying things like, "How much weight can the foundation hold?" I said, "Concrete is concrete." But, no, I found out that they had to calculate things like the height of the house, how many stories it would have, and what the roof would weigh when it was finished. They had to check all those things before they even started the foundation. Why? Because if there are twenty tons weighing on the foundation, they have to put in enough reinforced steel so that when the weight sits on it, it doesn't crack. The foundation has to have the first priority because everything else will be built on it.

THE FOUNDATION HAS TO HAVE THE FIRST PRIORITY BECAUSE EVERYTHING ELSE WILL BE BUILT ON IT.

Again, when God made the male first, He wasn't saying that the male is more important than the female. He was saying that the male has a specific responsibility. He has a purpose to fulfill that is just like the foundation. Even though the foundation is important, it's not more important than the other parts of the building. The foundation can't perform all the functions itself. For example, it cannot protect the occupants from the weather. You can walk around saying, "I have a $500,000 foundation here." Isn't that nice—solid concrete. But then the rain comes. The foundation can't keep you dry; only the roof can. It's the same way with the human family. The foundation is crucial, but the rest of the family is essential, also.

Remember that the foundation is often hidden. I don't see the foundation of my house anymore, even though I was involved in discussions about it and watched it being dug and poured. I know it's there, because I saw it being put in. Today, I walk on the foundation all the time, but I never see it. The foundation is meant to be solid, dependable, but not necessarily seen.

Many of you men need to live like the foundation you were created to be—just be there and keep the home steady so that your wife and children can always lean on you and know that you aren't going to crack. Many young boys with

WHEN A NEGATIVE HISTORY PREDICTS YOUR FUTURE, YOUR PRESENT IS IN TROUBLE.

absentee fathers—men who are missing either physically or emotionally—are walking in mud instead of on concrete. These young boys are trying to find a foundation for their lives, but there's mud all over them, because there's just

no place where they can stand on solid ground. Their foundations are missing. Then, when they grow up, they will go out and try to become foundations themselves. The only problem is, they were never shown what a true foundation is.

I once heard the statement, "A young boy becomes a man when his father tells him he's a man." Many young boys never had a father to tell them who they are. The purpose of the male-man is to give foundation to the structure of life.

I'm praying that God will raise up some strong foundational men. Men who will stand by their wives and stand with their children and be there as a stabilizer. Men whose families will feel secure in their strength. It doesn't matter what your father was—you can be a strong foundation by becoming the man God created you to be.

I was speaking about this topic in Barbados recently, and a young man said to me, "But you don't understand the history of the Afro-Caribbean man. I inherited my granddaddy and great-granddaddy's legacy, you know." I said, "Hold it right there. Whenever a negative history predicts your future, your present is in trouble. Don't come and tell me that you have to repeat your history. What we are about is *creating* history. We need to create a new history for all our children's children." And then I told him, "It doesn't matter who your grandfather was. The important issue is what your *grandchildren* are going to say about you."

Solomon said, *"A good man leaves an inheritance for his children's children"* (Prov. 13:22). I like that. A good man doesn't think about the past. He thinks about the future. A good man doesn't leave an inheritance of just money and land. That's not the only inheritance Solomon was talking about. He was talking about a heritage, something to stand on, something to lean on throughout life.

Maybe when you were growing up, your father left when things got tough. You think you need to do the same thing now that you have a family. Let me tell you: if you have a little boy, and you leave, you'll teach him the same thing your father taught you. It doesn't stop. It causes a perpetual cycle of destruction. We have to stop this cycle by getting back to God's Manual and getting on course again.

2. The Male's Position

Man's priority in creation not only means that he was designed to be the foundation of the human family, but also that he was the first to be positioned on earth according to God's purposes. He was the first to have a relationship with God, to experience God's creation, and to receive God's instructions.

In the Garden

The male was placed in the environment in which he was meant to carry out his purpose: *"Now the LORD God had planted a garden in the east, in Eden; and there he put the man he had formed"* (Gen. 2:8). This point is very, very crucial. God put the man in the environment in which he was supposed to remain in order to fulfill his reason for being. What was this environment like?

A PLACE OF HEAVEN ON EARTH

"Eden" comes from a Hebrew word meaning "delicate," "delight," or "pleasure." The word for *"garden"* means "an enclosure" or something "fenced in." This was more than an ordinary garden. All that was influencing heaven influenced that particular location on earth. God did not start by placing man over the entire earth or by placing him just anywhere on the earth. He placed man at the spot called Eden, where there was a glory connection between the seen and the unseen. There was glory flowing back and forth from this particular place on earth.

The Garden can be considered God's "incubator" for His new offspring. Sometimes a newborn baby is placed in an incubator so that he can become physically acclimated to his environment. In a sense, man was in **THE PRIMARY PURPOSE OF THE MALE IS TO BE IN GOD'S PRESENCE.** God all along, since he was *"chosen ...before the foundation of the world"* (Eph. 1:4 KJV). It was as if man was so used to the environment of being in God that God chose a special place on the planet and put His anointing on it for the sake of the man when He put him on the earth. In this way, the transition wouldn't be a strain on him. He could live in a controlled environment—a little spot of heaven on earth.

A PLACE OF GOD'S CONTINUAL PRESENCE

A central reason that God placed the male in the Garden was so that he could be in His presence all the time. He could walk and talk with the Lord in the cool of the day. He could hear God's voice. This was a place where communion, fellowship, and oneness with God was always intact.

A manufacturer will always position a part in the location where it can best carry out its purpose. Similarly, we can conclude from what we've learned about the environment of the Garden that the primary purpose of the male-man is to be in God's presence. The male is not wired to function outside the presence of the Lord.

Here's the significance: God never intended for Adam to move from the Garden. He intended for the *Garden to move over the earth.* God wanted Adam to take the presence of the Garden and spread it throughout the world. This is what He meant when He told Adam to have dominion over the earth. This is still God's purpose. As it says in Isaiah 11:9, *"The earth will be full of the knowledge of the LORD, as the waters cover the sea."* Adam could fulfill this purpose only if he was in constant communion with the God of the Garden.

> **GOD DIDN'T INTEND FOR ADAM TO MOVE FROM THE GARDEN. HE INTENDED FOR THE GARDEN TO MOVE OVER THE EARTH.**

If a man is not living in the presence of God, he might be moving, but he is not really functioning. Outside the presence of God, he's a dangerous, uncontrolled beast. Paul said that a man without God is a creature without conscience. (See Romans 1:28–32.) You can't trust the perspective of a man who doesn't know God. You cannot totally trust the perspective of one who is just beginning to get to know God either, because he's still getting used to the Presence.

It is only by continually being in God's presence that our minds and hearts can be renewed. We need to learn to walk *"in step with the Spirit"* (Gal. 5:25), rather than in step with our own ideas about life. As the prophet Jeremiah said, *"The heart is deceitful above all things and beyond cure. Who can understand it?"* (Jer. 17:9).

The problem with many of us men is that we think we don't need God when, in fact, He's the first thing we need. I'm amazed when I observe men trying to make it without God. They may appear to be making it, but they aren't. They're not fulfilling their true purpose. Often, the "making it" is just an external face they put on to keep people from seeing the way things really are. If you knew what was truly going on in their lives, you'd know they weren't making it.

We should never doubt our need of God. What was the first thing that God gave the male? He didn't give him a woman, a job, or even a command; He gave him His presence.

It isn't enough just to go to church. We need to be in touch with Him constantly, hearing His voice, listening to His commands, following His direction. Why? Because our inner beings need to be strengthened (Eph. 3:16), and because we are responsible for leading those for whom we are accountable. That's why God gave Adam Himself before He gave him anyone or anything else.

God built into the male a need for His presence. That is why all men are searching for God in one way or another, whether they acknowledge it or not. It doesn't matter if they are Buddhists, Hindus, Muslims, Unitarians, even satanists. No matter who they are, they are searching for the same Person. Men will always find some kind of religion, even if they call it atheism. They have a hunger to believe in something or someone greater than themselves.

That passion to find God's presence is what produces cults. It's the male-man's cry for God. **ALL MEN ARE SEARCHING FOR GOD IN ONE WAY OR ANOTHER.** Deep in your heart, you really want God, young man. You really want God, older man. You're trying everything else, but you're really looking for God. It's built into you. You can have fame, authority, influence, money, and everything else, but there is still something missing in your life, my friend. I know what it is. You're looking for God.

Some of you reading this book ran around in the world for a while and eventually came back to God. You ran far and wide trying to get away from Him. You slept with everybody, drank everything, sniffed everything. And now look at you—you're right back in God's presence, and you're glad you found what you were looking for all the time. It's good to come back to the One whom you've been looking for. If this is your experience, you likely don't have any fear of preaching the Gospel—because you know exactly what men are looking for. Oh, they hide behind all kinds of things—briefcases, fancy cars, stubbornness, swearing, fighting, drinking—but deep in their hearts, they're looking for God. And you can tell them, "When you're finished searching, I'll be right here. I'll lead you to God," because you've been where they are.

Wouldn't it be great for a family to have a husband or father in the home whom they could know was in touch with God so that they could get direction for their lives? The key is relationship. God put the male in the Garden because He wanted him always to be related to Him in fellowship and communion.

A Place of Training

God's directive to man was, *"Fill the earth and subdue it"* (Gen. 1:28). Yet God told the male, in essence, "Have dominion over this spot right here so that you become used to ruling on a smaller scale at first." The implication is that God intended for this man to grow in dominion ability by learning to dominate the area in which he was initially placed. If you've been faithful over a little, then your rulership will be expanded to much more. (See Matthew 25:14–23.)

God is so good to us. He doesn't give us more than we can handle. He always gives us just enough to train us for the rest. I hope you understand this principle. God will always give you just **GOD ALWAYS** enough so that you can get used to the **GIVES US JUST** idea of more. Many of us want everything **ENOUGH TO** right now. We short-circuit God's plan **TRAIN US FOR** because we grasp for everything at once. **THE FUTURE.** God is saying, in effect, "You'll get everything, but not right at this moment. You have not yet developed the character and the experience and the exercising of your potential to enable you to handle more."

The story of the Prodigal Son is a case in point. (See Luke 15:11–32.) The son *demanded* from his father what was coming to him. He really always had everything, since he was a beloved son of his father and would receive his inheritance. However, his father wanted him to work with him first in the family business. He wanted him to gain experience by helping to run the estate and by learning responsibility. Then he would be able to handle whatever difficulties he might face in the future.

You should find out what God has qualified you for, then ask for that. If you receive more than you are qualified for, then what you receive may well disqualify you because you're not prepared for it.

So God placed the male in Eden in order to prepare him. Yet, as we'll see, the man couldn't even handle the Garden. Imagine if he had had the whole earth to begin with! It's dangerous to have everything, all at once. I thank God for the process He uses in our lives. God doesn't just promote us. He qualifies us for promotion. Our question of Him should not be, "God, when will you promote me?" but "God, am I ready for promotion?"

3. THE MALE'S ASSIGNMENT

The third thing that determines a man's purpose is his assignment. *Assignment* means a task or something that has been entrusted to you to do. The responsibilities with which God has entrusted the male are very clear, and they indicate his purpose. What God gave Adam to do still holds true for men today because God is a God of purpose and has a reason for everything He does. He is teaching us His plan for mankind in the account of Creation.

VISIONARY AND LEADER

"The LORD God took the man and put him in the Garden of Eden to work it and take care of it. And the LORD God commanded the man" (Gen. 2:15–16). Whom did the Lord command? He commanded the male-man. What did He tell him? *"You are free to eat from any tree in the garden; but you must not eat from the tree of the knowledge of good and evil, for when you eat of it you will surely die"* (vv. 16–17). The male, being first, received all the information, all the revelation, all the communication from God. God wanted him to be the initial recipient of His plan for mankind. He showed him the whole Garden, the whole environment of Eden, a vision of everything He had created, and then He gave him instructions for living.

The female wasn't formed until after the events of the above Scripture passage. Therefore, the male received all

82

that information alone. He was in charge alone. He was responsible alone. He was a leader alone. Thus, the male was given the charge of being the visionary and leader, the one who would guide those who came after him in the ways of God. You will see as we go along that everything that is necessary to lead the family is built into the male.

This doesn't mean that women don't also have the capacity to be visionaries and leaders. However, the male is the one to whom God first entrusted His plans and purposes for the world. He was a leader before the woman was created. God gave the man the job of passing along what He had communicated to Him. This is still His purpose for males in the family and in society.

This fact is very important for men to understand. They have been entrusted with God's purposes. The male is to be responsible for everything under his jurisdiction. This is a serious thing. If something goes wrong in your family, you are accountable. You may say, as Adam told God when mankind fell, "But the woman...." (See Genesis 3:12.) No, not the woman—you are responsible. God went straight to Adam even though Eve was the one who first ate the fruit. When God asked him, *"Where are you?"* (v. 9), the question was not one of location, but of position. "You are not fulfilling your purpose of leadership, Adam. What has happened to your family?"

EVERYTHING THAT IS NECESSARY TO LEAD THE FAMILY IS BUILT INTO THE MALE.

The male's purpose was not chosen by the male but by God. Whatever your purpose, that's where your position comes from. Purpose, rather than social expectation, should determine position. The male is not elected the head of the family. You don't canvas for votes in the family to become the head of the home. If you are a man, you *are* the head of the family. You are the responsible one, whether you like it or not. If you run from this responsibility, it will run after you, because it's not just a role; it's a God-given purpose. However, it needs to be understood in light of God's Word and not in the context of society's definition of what head of the household means. We'll talk more about this in the next chapter.

TEACHER

God told Adam, in effect, "This is My command: 'Do not eat of the tree in the middle of the Garden, the Tree of Knowledge of Good and Evil.'" He didn't tell this to Eve. He told it only to Adam, which means that it was the man's responsibility to teach and guide her in the Word of God.

If I were the first one to discover something, and then someone else were to show up on the scene needing to know the information, what would that make me? It would make me the teacher. The fact that I was there first and had all the information would put me in that position. Likewise, the male was given the purpose of being the teacher, not because he's smarter, but because he was first. This is the pattern that God established. Again, this doesn't mean that women are unable to teach, but that God intended men to be primarily responsible for teaching His ways.

In Genesis 3, satan came to tempt Eve, and he asked her, "Didn't God say you shouldn't eat from any of these trees?" (See verse 1.) Eve's answer was **GOD INTENDED MEN TO BE PRIMARILY RESPONSIBLE FOR TEACHING HIS WAYS.** based on what she had heard from Adam, not from God, because Adam had been the one God instructed. She said, "No; we can eat of all the trees except the one that's called the Tree of Knowledge of Good and Evil. We can't even touch it." (See verses 2–3.) Eve learned that from her teacher. Perhaps she added the embellishment, or perhaps Adam did; it's not clear. But the point is that it was Adam's job to teach her God's instructions.

Ephesians 5 tells us that Jesus Himself teaches His bride, the church, *"by the washing with water through the word"* (v. 26). Christ is a teacher, and *"husbands ought to love their wives...just as Christ loved the church"* (vv. 28,

25). To this very day, God has not changed His purpose. The male must be responsible for godly instruction. I'm not talking about the way things are right now. I'm talking about what is supposed to be. God expects males to reveal His will and His Word to females. However, in our day, the males have lost God's will so badly that God is telling the females directly. He can do this because the woman has a spirit-man within her and has her own relationship with God. Yet God desires men to be spiritual leaders.

CULTIVATOR

What assignments did God give the male in regard to the Garden? The Bible says, *"The LORD God took the man and put him in the Garden of Eden to work* [*"cultivate"* NAS] *it"* (Gen. 2:15). So one of the male's responsibilities is to work or cultivate. Let's look first at the idea of the man *cultivating* the Garden.

The nature of the work the male was given to do was not mindless labor—it was cultivation. I wish every man could take hold of this truth. To *cultivate* means to make something grow and produce a greater yield. This means that, if you are a man, your purpose is to cultivate everything around you. *Cultivate* also means to make something fruitful, to develop it into its perfection. The man is to be a developer and a fruit producer. He is to be a source of fruitfulness. God gave this assignment to the male before the female was created, and before the first child was born. Therefore, the purpose of the male-man is to develop and cultivate both people and things to God's glory.

PROVIDER

Now let's look at the idea of the man *working* the Garden. Cultivation involves both creativity and effort. These two things are the nature of true work.

Men, I want to introduce you to one of your primary purposes. It is very simple, nothing complicated. You don't have to try to be Batman. You don't have to compete with

Arnold Schwarzenegger or anybody else. You don't have to have big muscles. You can weigh 110 pounds and still fulfill your purpose—no problem. God gave you the assignment of work.

Now, I hear somebody saying, "I'm so mad at Adam. Because Adam sinned, now I have to go to work." I have news for you: work was given to the man in Genesis 2, before the Fall. In other words, work is not a curse, my friend. Let me tell you the primary reason God gave you work. It is given in Genesis 2:2–3:

> *By the seventh day God had finished the work he had been doing; so on the seventh day he rested from all his work. And God blessed the seventh day and made it holy, because on it he rested from all the work of creating that he had done.*

God Himself worked when He created the world, and He still works to carry out His purposes. For example, Paul said in Philippians 2:13, *"It is God who works in you to will and to act according to his good purpose."* Because you are made in God's image and likeness, you are designed to work. Yet remember that work is meant to include creativity and cultivation, not drudgery. It is also supposed to be kept in its proper place. In Genesis 2, the Bible says that God worked hard and completed His work, so that He stopped His work and rested. He didn't burn the midnight oil or work seven days a week just for the sake of working. He stopped working when it was appropriate. He told us to do the same. (See Exodus 20:9–10.)

WORK EXPOSES YOUR POTENTIAL.

What is the significance of work? *Work exposes your potential.* You cannot show what you have inside unless demands are made on it, and demands are placed on it by work.

God gave the male work because it is related to his purpose. His purpose is to stay in the presence of the Lord and learn to rule and manage what God has given him to do. In this way, he can eventually fulfill God's complete plan for him, which is to dominate the earth.

God gave the male work not only because it exposes his potential and allows him to reflect God's nature, but also because it enables him to provide for those for whom he is responsible in his position as visionary and leader. *Provide* comes from a Latin word meaning "to see ahead." The male should be a visionary. He should have a vision for his life, and he should work to see that it is accomplished—for himself, his family, and others under his care. A male is designed for this purpose of provider. In general, he's built physically stronger than the female, particularly in his upper body, because of God's command that he work.

GOD HAS EQUIPPED YOU TO CARRY OUT EVERY PURPOSE AND FUNCTION YOU HAVE BEEN GIVEN.

PROTECTOR

"The LORD God took the man and put him in the Garden of Eden to...take care of it" (Gen. 2:15). The next responsibility the male was given was to *"take care"* of the Garden. I would include under this responsibility *guarding* and *protecting* the Garden and everything in it. That included the plants, the animals, even the woman who would be created and live in the Garden. God never told the woman to protect anything. Why? Because the woman is one of the things the man is supposed to protect.

I once asked God, "Lord, with all the responsibilities you gave us men, how do we know we can fulfill them?" His answer was very, very simple. He said, "Whatever I call for, I provide for." It is so true. We are designed as men to fulfill these functions.

God designed the male to protect everything that is in his care and under his covering, so that the male is a natural protector. The man is built in every way to protect. His physical frame is evidence of that, but so is his mental capacity. The way he is structured psychologically is designed to protect. We will discuss this idea more in the chapter entitled, "The Male as Provider and Protector." Rest assured that, as a male, God has equipped you to carry out every purpose and function you have been given.

There's a final aspect of the male as both provider and protector that I want you to recognize. Before the woman came, God gave the man one last responsibility:

> *Now the* LORD *God had formed out of the ground all the beasts of the field and all the birds of the air. He brought them to the man to see what he would name them; and whatever the man called each living creature, that was its name. So the man gave names to all the livestock, the birds of the air and all the beasts of the field.* (Gen. 2:19–20)

Did you know that the Hebrew concept of naming things actually means to possess them? This idea is very important in the Bible. Why did God tell the male-man to name the animals? Why didn't God name them Himself? It is because whatever you name, you own. Whatever you name, you control. Very interesting. That's why God named the male.

God called us His children because He always wants to have rights to us. We belong to Him. *"In him we live and move and have our being"* (Acts 17:28). No one else has a right to you because God named you. Do you understand that this is why satan has no legal rights to you? You are already named, so he can't name you.

This idea is why God made sure that Mary and Joseph didn't name Jesus. He personally named His Son. Why? He didn't want Jesus' earthly parents to possess Him. He knew that the day would come when Jesus would reach twelve years of age and His mother would ask Him, "Why did you leave us, Son?" and He would have to say, *"'I must be about My Father's business.'* He named Me. You didn't name Me." (See Luke 2:48–49 NKJV.)

Can I take you one step further? This is why God did not name the woman. Now, men, that's a lot of weight on our shoulders. God chose not to name the female. He wanted the man to be totally responsible for her. This is why, in marriage, a woman has traditionally taken her husband's name. It is to signify that he is responsible for her.

Real men are very careful about naming things, because they know the truth of this principle: what you name, you claim; and what you claim, you have the responsibility for. Young men, don't be so quick to give your name away, because whomever you give your name to, you have to cherish and love; care for and secure; and protect and work for. Young women, the next time a man comes to you and wants to give you his name, see if you want to be claimed.

GOD WANTED THE MAN TO BE TOTALLY RESPONSIBLE FOR THE WOMAN.

Check him out. Say, "Can you sustain me? Can you supply what I need?" I'm not referring to just money. I'm talking about comfort, knowledge, intellectual stimulation, protection, security. Ask him, "Can you provide these things for me?" Many men have money, but they don't have much sense. You don't want a rich fool. You want a real male-man.

SIX ASPECTS OF THE MALE'S ASSIGNMENT

The male's assignment has revealed six specific purposes that God created the man to fulfill: *visionary, leader, teacher, cultivator, provider, and protector.* If every man could live out these six things, he would begin to realize his true purpose as a male. Any man who does not understand these elements will experience great frustration—which some of you are experiencing right now. To be a strong man means to discover, understand, and fulfill these basic aspects of purpose. These areas are so crucial that we will look at them in more detail in later chapters.

It is important to realize that although some of the traditional male roles reflect these purposes, much of the gender confusion and many of the other problems we're having in our societies have come from our interpretation of these roles. For example, as we saw, being a provider means supplying not only financial support but also emotional and intellectual support. A man whose wife makes more money than he does but who is doing his utmost to work a job and to fulfill these needs can still be a good provider. We need to focus on God's purpose, rather than roles. God will enable men to fulfill their true purpose as they look to Him for guidance and help.

I also want to emphasize that because these areas have to do with the male's purpose, the ability to fulfill them is already in his nature. Many people don't understand how close the relationship is between purpose and nature. The nature of a man reveals who he is and how he functions.

A COMPLETE MAN IS STILL ALONE

All these purposes for the male were given to him by God *before* the creation of the female. This is a vital point to remember: it is the man who is already living and working in his purposes about which God says, *"It is not good for the man to be alone. I will make a helper suitable for him"* (Gen. 2:18). You might not think that a man who has a close relationship with God, who understands his role as foundation, who has been given the vision, who can lead, teach, cultivate, provide, and protect, needs anyone else. Yet even a man who knows and lives in his purpose is not complete, according to God. The male needs a companion, someone to be his helper—not as a subordinate or a sidekick, but as an equal partner with a complementary purpose. This is as true for single men as it is for married men. Men need women as fellow workers and colleagues in this world if they are to fulfill their purpose in life.

> **THE MALE NEEDS A COMPANION—NOT AS A SUBORDINATE OR A SIDEKICK, BUT AS AN EQUAL PARTNER.**

THE CREATION OF THE FEMALE

When God placed the spirit-man in the male, God and man still maintained a relationship of love through their spirits. However, because the man now had a physical body, he also needed someone with whom he could share his life on earth, someone with whom he could express emotional and physical love.

Genesis 2:20 tells us, *"So the man gave names to all the livestock, the birds of the air and all the beasts of the field.*

But for Adam no suitable helper was found." God presented every animal to the man, but none was suitable for him. There was no one to whom he could re-late, no one who could help him in his proprietorship of the earth. So God said, in effect, "It's not good for man to be alone in one body." It is impossible for love to love alone. So God created the woman, the female-man. The primary purpose of the female was to receive love from the male, just as God's major purpose for creating the spirit-man was to have a relationship of love with mankind. Having dominion over the earth was secondary.

> **MALE AND FEMALE ARE OF THE SAME SUBSTANCE.**

1. OF THE SAME SUBSTANCE AND ESSENCE AS THE MALE

The method that God used to create the female is significant to our understanding of the relationship between males and females:

> *The LORD God caused the man to fall into a deep sleep; and while he was sleeping, he took one of the man's ribs and closed up the place with flesh. Then the LORD God made a woman from the rib he had taken out of the man, and he brought her to the man.* (Gen. 2:21–22)

Just as God had drawn man from Himself and created him as a spiritual being, He drew the woman out of the man and made her a physical being. This parallel in creation illustrates the oneness and mutual love that God and man and male and female were created to have.

The word *"rib"* in Genesis 2:22 is the Hebrew word *tsela.* It does not necessarily mean a rib as we understand the word. It could mean "side" or "chamber." The Scripture is telling us that God drew the woman from a part of the man. Why? It is because the receiver has to be exactly like the giver. Just as man needed to be spirit in order to receive love from God and be in relationship with Him, the woman needed to be of the same essence as the man in order to receive love from him and be in relationship with him.

That is why God did not go back to the soil to fashion another house when He formed the female. If He had done that, she would not have been the exact duplicate of the man. She would not have been made of the essence of the male, the way humanity was made of the essence of God. So God took just what was needed from the male to make an exact replica, and He created the woman.

Now, while males and females are of the same essence, and while the woman is a replica of the man, God actually made them using different methods. The Bible says that the man was *"formed"* of the dust of the earth (Gen. 2:7). The Hebrew word for *"formed"* is *yatsar,* meaning to "mold," as a potter molds clay. However, the Bible says that God *"made"* the woman (v. 22). The Hebrew word for *"made"* is *banah,* which means to "build" or "construct."

So there was this beautiful structuring in the creation of woman. When God had finished making her, she was just like the man. She was so much in likeness to him that, when God presented her to him, his first words were, *"This is now bone of my bones and flesh of my flesh; she shall be called 'woman,' for she was taken out of man"* (v. 23). And she became his wife. The man's words are both beautiful and instructive. Something that is built has the same components as the material from which it is made or from which it comes. Therefore, God built the female out of the part that He took from the male so that they would be made of exactly the same substance.

2. THE MALE'S PERFECT COMPLEMENT

The female-man is the perfect complement to the male-man. Because the woman came from the man, the man is essentially the giver, and the woman is essentially the receiver. God fashioned the woman to be the receiver. If you look at the way the female body is made, she is a receiver from A to Z. Her receiving complements the male's giving. The woman is like the man because the receiver has to be of the same essence as the giver. However, in order for the woman to be the receiver, she also has to be different from the man.

Though the woman was built to be like the man, she is also a distinct creation. This fact is highlighted in her physical difference from the man in that she is able to bear children. You could say that a woman is a "wombed man." She is a man with a womb. She is still the same as a male, but she has certain differences. These differences are complementary in nature and are de- **EVE WAS GOD'S IDEA FOR ADAM.** signed so that the male and female can fulfill one another's emotional and physical needs while they are spiritually nourished by God and His love—and so that together they can fulfill their mandate to have dominion over the world. Therefore, men and women were created with complementary designs that reflect their individual roles in the larger purposes for which they were created.

3. THE MALE'S GOD-GIVEN COMPANION

When God said, *"It is not good for the man to be alone. I will make a helper suitable for him"* (Gen. 2:18), He was saying, in essence, "I will make someone who will solve the male's aloneness."

Now, Adam did not go looking for a wife. She was God's idea for him. Adam was so busy doing what God had told him to do that he didn't even know he needed a woman. God had to tell him, "Man, it's not good for you to be alone." Note that God didn't say Adam was lonely. There is a difference between "being alone" and "being lonely."

You can be lonely in a crowd, but you can be alone and be as happy as a lark. There is nothing wrong with being alone at times. The Bible tells us that it's important to be alone and quiet before the Lord. Jesus often made it a point to go off by Himself in order to pray and rest. Being alone can be healthy, but loneliness is a disease.

Have you noticed that people who are suffering from loneliness never can go into their houses and just sit down in the quiet? As soon as they get inside, they run for the television and click it on. They have to have something going on that will occupy their minds. When they can't find anything on television that they like, then they run to their cassette or CD players. When they become bored with music, they try something else. They keep doing things in order to stay occupied. Why? Because they're not comfortable with themselves. They can't stand being alone.

Some of you single men and women are afraid of being alone. When you hit age twenty-five, you begin to think you're past your prime, and so you say to yourselves, "I'm never going to get married. I'd better latch onto the first thing that comes along." That's the reason many people marry spouses who aren't right for them. Do you know what the problem is? They haven't learned what it means to be a whole person.

SEEK FIRST THE KINGDOM, AND YOUR MATE WILL BE ADDED TO YOU.

Adam was so together as a man that he didn't even know he was alone. He was busy obeying God's Word; he was so occupied with dominating, ruling, and subduing; he was so lost in what he was doing, that he didn't know he needed somebody. But most of us do the reverse. We don't have time for God because we're busy trying to find a mate.

Some people run from church to church looking for a spouse. They think we preachers don't know what they're up to. They don't go to church to worship God; instead, they walk around checking out the opposite sex. They say, "Huh, that's a nice one over there. Really cool." Instead, they're supposed to be getting themselves together so they can be ready for the one whom God is preparing for them. Become so preoccupied and consumed by God that you don't walk around with a passion that's looking for a place to happen.

Adam was so prepared for Eve that when he saw her, all he said was, "Woooo-man!" But you see, he didn't go looking for her. Jesus talked about the attitude we should have when He said, in effect, "Don't worry about what you're going to eat, what you're going to wear, or whom you're going to marry. Seek first the kingdom of God. Become immersed in His righteousness. Then your mate will be added to you." (See Matthew 6:31–33.)

Become like Adam—get lost in the garden of God's righteousness. Get lost in God, because when He brings you a spouse, you had better understand His ways. Adam was so busy following the command of God that, when his mate came along, he was ready, and it was the right time for him.

4. THE MALE'S "SUITABLE HELPER"

So the woman was God's idea. He made the woman specifically so that the man could have somebody with whom to enjoy creation and share the dominion of the earth.

God said, *"I will make a helper suitable for him"* (Gen. 2:18). The King James Version uses the words *"help meet"* rather than *"helper suitable"* as in the *New International Version* or *"helper comparable"* as in the *New King James Version.* *"Help meet"* is not a Hebrew expression, and it's not a holy phrase. When King James ordered an English translation of the Scriptures at the beginning of the seventeenth century, the translators used the words that were common at the time to explain various concepts. *Helpmeet* or *helpmate* are words that developed in the English language based on this King James translation, and they have remained in the language. However, because our use of words has changed, they do not fully capture the concept the Bible is conveying here about the role of the woman.

EVERYTHING ABOUT THE WOMAN IS DESIGNED TO HELP.

The woman is not just someone who helps here and there while the men do the real work. *"Meet"* actually means "fit"—something that is suitable, compatible, or comparable. This means that females are a perfect match for males in fulfilling God's purposes.

God designed the woman to fulfill her purpose of being a compatible helper for the man. Everything in her is designed to help. Now, the last thing many men want women to believe is that they need their help. Yet God announced from the beginning that a man needs a woman's help. Again, this is true for all men, not just married men. Males need females not only in the family, but in society, in all of life.

One of the reasons our nations are so troubled is that males don't know their own purpose or the purpose of females. Many men don't run their homes properly because they walk around saying, "I am the final authority." They don't realize that the women God gave them are a blessing and that they are there to help them carry out their vision. If you as a man—whether married or single—believe that you don't need women, you are missing an important aspect of your existence.

Many males with whom I've been in contact over the years believe that women were put on earth by God to destroy them. They think that everything a woman does is conniving and scheming. They don't understand the true nature and purpose of women. If you don't understand why something is the way it is, you will become suspicious of its nature.

SOMETIMES A WOMAN'S HELP IS SEEN AS A THREAT.

For example, sometimes the help that a woman brings a man is interpreted as a threat. He sees it as her trying to take his position. Many men don't understand the value of the woman in her purpose as helper. So when a woman wants to be a part of what a man is doing, he thinks she's interfering. Yet she is the way she is because of why she was created. She wants to know what you're doing that she can't help with. What could be so secretive, so deep?

Women who are kept at a distance by men keep on reaching out, trying to help, but the men see them as a nuisance and say, "Mind your own business. This is a man's world; find your place." Well, her place is right next to you, helping you. If she can't help you, she will help something—or someone—else.

Some of these precious women are so talented, so experienced in all kinds of things. They have excellent educations, are very accomplished, and are ready to help their husbands or other males in any way they can, but the men get flippant with them because they don't understand God's plan.

One of the reasons for this is that some men can't handle the presence of a complete woman. My friend, you're not a strong man until you can handle the weight of a real woman—I'm talking about a *real* woman. Some women are off balance. However, there are some real women in the world, and it takes a real man to be a support for them. Many women are loaded with gifts and anointing. Because women have such an awesome capability to help, most men feel powerless when their helper shows up. Why? Because they were never taught what a man is all about and don't know how to fulfill their own purpose.

> YOU'RE NOT A STRONG MAN UNTIL YOU CAN HANDLE THE WEIGHT OF A REAL WOMAN.

Do you ever wonder why the church is so filled with women? Often, it is because they don't have anything to help with at home. Do you know why your wife leaves you to go to church? You don't have any vision in the home, so she goes to church and helps this minister with his vision. She helps in children's church or in Sunday school because she has a need to contribute.

Some women even help men do wrong things if they can't find men doing right things. A man may tell a woman, "You wait in the car while I rip off this store," and she feels good about it, because she is doing something to help him. She feels worthy. She feels valuable to this man. Some women carry drugs and do deals for their kingpin boyfriends. Do you wonder how they can do that? In a warped way, they are seeking to be fulfilled, to have their needs met.

THE ABUSE OF PURPOSE

Remember one of our principles: where purpose is not known, abuse is inevitable? When men and women misunderstand their purposes, then these purposes will be abused in some way. It is a misunderstanding of purpose that has pulled men and women away from God's original design in creation. This has resulted in a false idea of dominion and of the relationship between males and females that is causing confusion and conflict between them. As long as we allow this to continue, we won't live fulfilled lives as men and women, and society will continue to decline.

It all started with the male and female thinking they knew their true purpose better than God did. Let's look next at the implications of this tragic misjudgment.

PRINCIPLES

1. The male's purpose was chosen by God.

2. The male was made to serve the needs of man (the spirit) on earth and to enable him to fulfill his purpose.

3. The purpose of the male may be summed up as *his priority, his position,* and *his assignment.*

4. The male's *priority* means that he was formed first in order to be the foundation of the human family.

5. The male's *position* means that he is to remain continually in God's presence. Without this, he cannot function in God's purposes.

6. God never intended for Adam to move from the Garden. He intended for the Garden of His presence to move over the earth.

7. God intended for the man to grow in dominion ability by first learning to rule the Garden.

8. The male's *assignment* includes six specific purposes he is meant to fulfill: visionary, leader, teacher, cultivator, provider, and protector.

9. God has designed and equipped the male to carry out every purpose and function he has been given.

10. God allowed Adam to name Eve because He wanted the male to be totally responsible for the female.

11. It is the male who is already living and working in his purposes about which God says, *"It is not good for the man to be alone. I will make a helper suitable for him"* (Gen. 2:18).

12. The female was drawn from the male and is made of the same essence as the male.

13. The female is the male's perfect complement and equal partner in the purposes of God.

14. The female is the male's God-given companion. She is God's idea for the man.

15. The female is the male's "suitable helper." Everything about her is designed to help the man.

5

DOMINION VERSUS DOMINATION

GOD CREATED MEN AND WOMEN TO DOMINATE
THE EARTH, NOT ONE ANOTHER.

Both males and females were created in God's image. The basis of their equality before God is that man, the spirit, resides within both of them. As physical beings they were created of the same essence, but differently—because each has been designed with specific purposes to fulfill. The different ways in which their dominion assignment is carried out does not affect their equality; it only reflects their distinct purposes, designs, and needs.

We saw in the previous chapter that the male was created to exercise dominion over the earth through his priority, position, and assignment. The female was created to help the male fulfill God's dominion purposes for mankind in both the earthly and spiritual realms. It is God's intention that, together, their individual strengths would combine to produce exponential

MEN AND WOMEN'S INDIVIDUAL STRENGTHS PRODUCE EXPONENTIAL RESULTS WHEN COMBINED.

results—outcomes much greater than either could accomplish alone. The woman adds to the man's power in living and working, so that the sum is far greater than its parts.

If males and females were created with perfectly complementary designs, why do men and women experience conflict and competition rather than cooperation? Why does the purpose of dominion over the earth seem more like a quest for domination of one sex over the other?

THE DOMINION PLAN ATTACKED

The third chapter of Genesis explains the source of the conflict. Sometime after God had instructed Adam that he could eat from any tree in the Garden except the Tree of Knowledge of Good and Evil, and Adam had passed this information along to Eve, the devil, in the form of a serpent, tempted Eve to eat from the tree.

GOD'S WORD QUESTIONED

I don't think this was the first time this animal had approached Eve. First, she didn't seem surprised to see him or to hear him speaking. I imagine she said to the serpent, "Oh, there you are again. What do you want this time?" Second, I believe they had talked earlier about God's instructions because of the way the devil phrased his crafty question: *"Did God **really** say, 'You must not eat from any tree in the garden'?"* (Gen. 3:1, emphasis added). His first tactic was to try to cast doubt on Eve's memory and understanding of what God had said.

GOD'S INTEGRITY ASSAULTED

Eve replied, *"We may eat fruit from the trees in the garden, but God did say, 'You must not eat fruit from the tree that is in the middle of the garden, and you must not touch it, or you will die'"* (vv. 2–3). She had most of her information correct, so the devil's next ploy was to try to undermine God's integrity in her eyes. *"'You will not surely die,' the serpent said to the woman. 'For God knows that when you eat of it your eyes will be opened, and you will be like God, knowing good and evil'"* (vv. 4–5). Eve succumbed to the temptation, Adam joined her of his own free will, and they both ate of the fruit of the tree. (See verse 6.)

THE SPIRIT-MAN REJECTED GOD'S PURPOSES

This decision resulted in the spiritual deaths of the man and the woman and their banishment from the Garden by God. (See verses 7–24.) Realize that it was the spirit-man—the responsible spiritual being—within both the male and female that made the fateful choice to eat the fruit in disobedience to God's command. This is why mankind's dilemma is a spiritual one.

When Adam and Eve rebelled, they immediately died a spiritual death—just as God had warned—and eventually the physical houses God had given them to live in on the earth also died. However, the spiritual death was the worse predicament of the two because it separated them from their former perfect fellowship with God. God still loved them, but they no longer had the same open channel to Him with which to receive His love. While they still retained elements of their creation in God's image, they no longer perfectly reflected the nature and character of their Creator.

OUR OWN IDEAS ABOUT OUR PURPOSE ARE LIMITED.

The devil had presented Adam and Eve with a big lie, and they had fallen for it, to their own sorrow. However, there was an underlying reason that mankind fell. To understand it, we need to look to our foundational principles of purpose:

- To discover the purpose of something, never ask the creation; ask the creator.

- We find our purpose only in the mind of our Maker.

In his temptation, the devil suggested to Adam and Eve an alternate purpose for their lives than God had already given them—they would know good and evil and supposedly become equal with God. Their wrong choice was based on their own ideas about their purpose, which were limited. In actuality, they were already "like God" in nature; they had been created in His image and reflected His glory. As for knowing good and evil, there were certain things God knew it was best for them not to know—or else He would have told them. If they were eventually to know them, God wanted them to be ready to receive this information so that it wouldn't harm them. Like the training in dominion rule they were meant to receive in the Garden, it would be best for them to learn it when they were prepared for it, so that they could handle it.

Adam and Eve fell because they became dissatisfied with their position and roles. They stopped looking to their Creator for their purpose and instead looked to themselves. They thought they knew their true purpose better than God did. Yet their rejection of God's plan brought them only heartache, because they were not meant to live independently from God and the purpose for which He had created them.

CONSEQUENCES OF LOST PURPOSE

Adam and Eve's tragic choice inevitably led to the fulfillment of another principle of purpose:

- Where purpose is not known (or rejected), abuse is inevitable.

Mankind's predicament can be summed up by a statement from the book of Romans: *"Although they claimed to be wise, they became fools"* (Rom. 1:22). Because the man and woman thought they knew what was best for themselves, they rejected their true reason for being and suffered the loss of many of the benefits and blessings God had given them. Inevitably, they also began to abuse each other's purposes. Men and women cannot function in true harmony and effectiveness outside God's plan.

BROKEN RELATIONSHIP BETWEEN MALES AND FEMALES

First, they lost their perfectly balanced relationship. Right away, we see conflict between them. When God asked Adam, *"Have you eaten from the tree that I commanded you not to eat from?"* Adam accused Eve, saying, *"The woman you put here with me—she gave me some fruit from the tree, and I ate it"* (Gen. 3:11–12). Feeling trapped, Eve tried to put the blame on the devil (v. 13). Yet God held each of them accountable because both were spiritual beings responsible to Him.

We see how Adam and Eve's decision to disobey God altered their relationship. God said that one of the consequences of their rejection of His purpose was that they would strive with one another. *"Your desire will be for your husband, and he will rule over you"* (Gen. 3:16). This statement emphasizes the fact that the male and female were originally created to rule together. They were designed to function together equally. God had said to them, *"Fill the earth and subdue it"* (Gen. 1:28). Both of them were supposed to be rulers—and that is still His plan.

After the Fall, both the man and the woman still ruled, but their relationship was distorted. Instead of equality, there was imbalance. The woman now had a longing after her husband that became controlling because it never seemed to be fulfilled. God also said that the man would develop an attitude of rulership over the woman. This was not part of God's plan; however, because of sin, the man's twisted perception of life would cause him to want to dominate the woman, and because of sin, the woman would continually desire to do anything to keep him.

BROKEN RELATIONSHIP WITH THE EARTH

Adam and Eve also lost their harmonious relationship with the earth. They forfeited their right to live in the controlled Garden environment in which they were to learn to have dominion over the earth, so that now they had to live under harsh conditions. God told Adam, *"Cursed is the ground because of you; through painful toil you will eat of it all the days of your life. It will produce thorns and thistles for you, and you will eat the plants of the field"* (Gen. 3:17–18). In other words, He was saying, "It is the earth that is really going to feel the impact of your disobedience. Because of this, you will have to struggle to survive in it."

In these consequences of sin—the broken relationship between Adam and Eve and the cursed ground—we see satan's scheme to try to undermine God's purposes of dominion. He was afraid of the power that would be released through a man and woman united in God's purposes. He also didn't want God's Garden spread over the world; he wanted his own fallen kingdom to prevail. Therefore, he sought to distort the relationship between males and females and limit the Garden by bringing an atmosphere of thorns and thistles to the rest of the earth. Jesus referred to the devil as the *"prince of this world"* (John 12:31) because, through the Fall, mankind became controlled by the *"spirit of the world"* (1 Cor. 2:12) rather than by God's Spirit.

SATAN IS AFRAID OF THE POWER OF A MAN AND WOMAN UNITED IN GOD'S PURPOSES.

Yet regardless of the Fall, God's purpose has never changed. His original design still stands. At the very hour of humanity's rejection of God's purpose, God promised a Redeemer who would save men and women from their fallen state and all its ramifications (Gen. 3:15). The Redeemer would restore the relationship and partnership of males and females. Jesus Christ is that Redeemer, and because of Him, men and women can return to God's original design for them. Christ came to redeem us from the spirit of the world so that we can fulfill God's purposes once again. We could call Him the legal representative of the Manufacturer. He came as an Authorized Dealer to restore the Manufacturer's specifications for His products. Purpose, peace, and potential can return to humanity. We can again have true dominion over the earth—but only through Christ.

Let's take a look at the problems of dominion and relationships that occur when we try to function without God's plan and without Christ's redemption and restoration.

A LOST UNDERSTANDING OF DOMINION

God created men and women to dominate the earth, not to dominate one another. The Fall, however, has caused us to lose the concept of what shared responsibility and respect is all about. Although both males and females reflect a controlling tendency in their own ways, I want to focus here on how it affects men. Throughout history, this tendency has particularly undermined the male's true purpose and has resulted in the widespread devaluing of women—preventing both men and women from fulfilling their purposes in God.

FEAR OF APPEARING WEAK

Much of a man's tendency to control comes from a false understanding of how his own nature is to function in dominion. Men have lost the knowledge of what God created them to be. They have mistaken power for strength. Let me explain what I mean.

Men have a deep desire to prove themselves strong. It is one of the underlying issues every male faces, whether he is a ten-year-old boy or a ninety-year-old man. Men's internal passion to prove their strength is inherent in their nature. Some call it "ego" or "manliness." Others call it "male pride" or "machismo." But all men have it in some form or another because of the purpose for which they were created. It is built in by God in order to give them the ability to fulfill their purpose of leading, protecting, and providing.

In its true form, the male ego is not negative, but positive. It is not evil, but godly. The problem is that the male's passion to prove his strength has been perverted and abused by satan and the sinful nature.

Because of this tendency to want to prove their strength, there is nothing more frightening to most men than to be perceived as weak. Again, this fear is a result of the Fall. Now that his true relationship with the female has been distorted, he feels vulnerable in this area of strength. He doesn't want to be perceived as being helpless or out of control by either males or females. This fear drives the man to feel as if he has to constantly prove himself. It is the source of his aggressive spirit. It is the source of his being overly competitive. It is also the source of some men's tendency toward violence.

A lot of men have muscle, but are weak in their minds, their hearts, their discipline, their responsibility, and their spirits. That is why they feel the need for excess muscle—to hide their weakness in these other areas. Many men don't understand why they have this desire for strength, so they compete with, fight, or even kill other men. They domineer their wives and cheat on them because they need to feel in control.

You can observe men in a barroom trying to build up each other's egos. "I showed my woman who's the boss in the family." "Yeah? Me, too. I tell her what she can and can't do." What they are really doing is lying to each other about their strength. They're fooling themselves. If you're wrong and I'm wrong, we'll feel better if we say we're right. Both of us are wrong, so we're comfortable together. We get together with all our foolishness and failures, and we encourage each other in order to give our failures dignity.

MANY MEN HAVE MUSCLE, BUT ARE WEAK IN THEIR MINDS, HEARTS, DISCIPLINE, RESPONSIBILITY, AND SPIRITS.

Now, you may think that you are different from other males. You may not outwardly fight with other men or try to control women, but you still struggle with the issue of proving yourself strong—in relationships, in work, in sports, in various aspects of life. If you ask women, they will agree that all men are alike in wanting to prove themselves strong—whether in positive or negative ways. And it's true. We have different personalities. We have different visions. We have different sizes and skin colors. We have different jobs and vocations. But we are all the same in this tendency. I can affirm this fact because I travel all over the world, and I see a similar pattern everywhere.

When I was in South Africa, I found that the men there, whether they are black or white, have the same tendency. In Ghana or in Nigeria, men are the same. The tendency can be found in Germany or in Italy. When I was in Canada, the women there had the same complaints about men that women do in the Bahamas. All over the world, women have the same complaints, no matter what language they speak or what nationality they are.

DOMINION VERSUS DOMINATION

POWER VERSUS STRENGTH

What men need is a picture of what a truly strong man looks like. A strong man is a man who understands his God-given strength. A strong man is a fully maximized man. Strength is ability, authority, capacity, potential. To be a strong man is to maximize all your potential for the purpose for which you were created. Jesus was the strongest Man who ever lived, yet He is also described as meek. Someone has said that meekness is power under control. That is what true strength is. It is power that is ready to be channeled into good and constructive purposes rather than reckless or selfish ones.

Remember that the purpose of something is the reason for which it was made, and its design is determined by that purpose. Strength was given to men to enable them to lead effectively. If you as a man understood your purpose, you would realize that you were not put in a leadership position because you are big, strong, or overbearing. You are put in that position because of your purpose. Your strength is meant to support that purpose.

I once heard a man on the Oprah Winfrey television show say, "I'm the head of my home, and if my wife doesn't like it, she can put up or shut up." I was sitting there thinking, "He needs a good session with me." Oprah asked him, "What makes you the head of the home?" and he said, "I'm the head of the home because I say so. I wear the pants in the family." Listen, if you're the man just because you wear the pants, you have a problem, because women wear pants, too.

Males didn't choose their position. God gave it to them. However, the problem is that many males have taken another position that they weren't given. If we voted for a man to become the president or prime minister of the country, but instead he took over by force and became a dictator, he'd be taking a position he wasn't given. The first position was given to him by legal authority; the other was seized.

Whenever you take your position by force, you've moved out of your legal standing. The difference between an elected head of state and a dictator is very simple. The first has authority and the second merely has power. To have authority means to have a right to govern. Therefore, if a man slaps his wife, kicks his children, and then says, "I'm the man of the house; I do what I want," that's an abuse of authority; it's merely wielding power over others. Whenever you abuse your power, you no longer have legitimate authority.

WHENEVER YOU TAKE YOUR POSITION BY FORCE, YOU'VE MOVED OUT OF YOUR LEGAL STANDING.

That is why, any time a man starts to dominate another human being, he is out of God's will. This principle applies to preachers, as well. Any minister who says to you, "You cannot go and visit anybody else's church," is someone to be wary of. He's beginning to dominate. And God says men were created to dominate the earth, not one another. When this occurs, and power is abused, then authority is forfeited.

A DISTORTED VIEW OF SUBMISSION

Many men's distorted understanding of strength can be seen in the way they view the concept of submission. Yet the passage in which this concept is found, Ephesians 5:22–23, contains something many people miss. It says, *"Wives, submit to your husbands as to the Lord. For the husband is the head of the wife as Christ is the head of the church."*

Let's first talk about the word *submission*. The definition of *submit* means to "willfully give your will to another." Submission has nothing to do with force or pressure. It's an act of the will. To submit is the *choice* of the person who is submitting, not the command of one who wants to be submitted to. Put another way, you cannot submit unless you want to, and no one can make you submit if you don't want to.

Any man who has to force a woman to submit does not deserve to be submitted to. He is no longer worthy of submission; he has become a slave driver. Do you know what makes a slave a slave? Force and fear. Those are the elements that are dominating too many homes. The Bible says, *"Perfect love drives out fear"* (1 John 4:18). This means that if a man has to make a woman afraid of him in order to force her to do something he wants done, then he doesn't know what love is.

The Scripture says, *"Wives submit to your husbands **as to the Lord**"* (Eph. 5:22, emphasis added). As long as a man is acting like the Lord, a woman should be in submission to him. I've never seen Jesus slap one of His children. I've never seen Jesus scream or swear at His people. No

SUBMISSION HAS NOTHING TO DO WITH FORCE. IT'S AN ACT OF THE WILL.

matter what we do to Jesus, He is ready to forgive us. This is how husbands need to treat their wives.

However, probably half of us men do not deserve our wives' submission. Jesus said to His church—His bride—*"Never will I leave you; never will I forsake you"* (Heb. 13:5). And yet, some men stay out all night, then come home and want their wives to cook for them. They forsake their wives and their children spiritually and emotionally, even financially, and they still want submission. That's a sin, men. You don't deserve submission. Submission is not dependent on what you say. It is dependent on how you live.

Do you believe in the Lord Jesus Christ as your personal Savior? All right, then. Before you were saved, did Jesus ever come to you and hold you up against the wall by your collar and say, "If you don't believe in Me, I'll send you straight to Hades?" He didn't do that. As a matter of fact, He probably waited a long time for you. When you were involved in all your foolish living, He didn't force you to accept Him. He didn't break down your door. He is very polite. He very quietly convicts people. He doesn't pressure us. He just shows us His love.

So, one day, you realized, "This love is overwhelming," and you accepted His love. You desired to follow Jesus. One of the things I love about Jesus is that He calls us to follow Him. He doesn't tie a rope around our necks and drag us.

He leads, and we follow. If we are willingly following somebody, we are not being forced against our wills.

Have you ever been on a guided tour of a cavern? The guide takes you down through these tunnels, and all you do is follow him. You submit to his authority because He knows the way through the dark tunnels. Of course, you can turn around anytime and go back, although you would probably walk into some walls and stub your toes and scrape your knees because you're not familiar with the cavern. However, the point is that you can turn around if you want to. And that is what God is trying to tell us.

JESUS DOESN'T TIE A ROPE AROUND OUR NECKS AND DRAG US. HE LEADS, AND WE FOLLOW.

Jesus doesn't force us to submit to Him. All He ever says to His disciples is, "Follow Me." This is exactly what husbands are supposed to say to their wives: "Honey, follow me." That's what submission is really about. Now, a woman may say, "I don't want to go where you're headed, buddy." You may be going toward making money and acquiring prestige while you ignore God and your family. You may be headed toward destroying your health with drugs and alcohol. You may be killing yourself with carousing and fooling around. Your wife doesn't want to follow you under those conditions, and you can't expect her to.

Do you know why we keep following Jesus? It is because He knows where He's going, He knows how to get there, He's the only Way there, and we like where He's going. Even more than that, His love draws us to Him. We love Jesus so much, we'll do anything He asks. Why do we love Him? It is not because He threatens us with a big hammer, saying, "If you sin, I'll kill you." He doesn't say that. He says, "If you sin, I am faithful and just to forgive you." (See 1 John 1:9.) Isn't it wonderful to follow Someone like that? Every time you slip, He picks you up and brushes you off. He doesn't talk about your past at all. We submit to Him because we love Him.

So the Scripture says, in essence, "Wives, submit to your husbands when they act like the Lord." Many wives, as well as husbands, don't understand this truth. For instance, suppose a husband comes home very drunk, and he goes up to his wife and says, "I want another drink! Go buy me another drink." Now, she's a precious Christian lady, so she says, "I don't think you should be dr—" He interrupts her, saying, "Shut up, woman! I'm the head of this home. The Bible says...." And he'll quote it, too! "The Bible says you're supposed to submit. Now, go and buy me a drink." She doesn't understand the true nature of submission, so she becomes afraid, takes some money, buys a bottle of something, and gives it to her husband—which he uses to abuse his health.

What she should do is look him in the face and say, "Honey, the Bible says that I should submit to you—when you act like the Lord. The Lord has never asked me to buy Him something that will destroy Him. And because I love you so much, honey, I won't go. I want you to live." Then, of course, she takes off running after she finishes saying that! But that is what the man needs to hear.

Situations in which people have unbelieving husbands or wives can be difficult, but the Bible tells us what to do under these circumstances. First Corinthians 7 says that if a woman holds to the standards of the Word of God, and her unbelieving husband agrees to stay with her, *"let her not leave him"* (v. 13 KJV). However, if he cannot live with her convictions, the Bible says, *"Let him depart"* (v. 15 KJV). In other words, if he can't live with her commitment to the Lord, the Bible tells her, "Let him go." You don't compromise your faith even for your spouse.

Some women allow their husbands to beat them half to death because they think that is being submissive. I have counseled many women who think this way. They come to my office badly battered, and ask, "What am I supposed to do?" I say, "Remove yourself from the premises." "But the Bible says to submit." "Yes, but not to a beating. You are to submit to the Lord. Until you see the Lord in the house, leave. You are not to be foolish enough just to sit there and let your life be put in jeopardy."

"Well, the Bible did say we have to suffer for Jesus." "My dear woman, your husband comes home totally drunk and beats you, and you're talking about suffering for Jesus? There is nothing in the Bible that says you should just stand there and suffer abuse. First Peter 2:19–20 says that if you suffer for the sake of the Gospel, that is true suffering. But if you suffer for the sake of your own sin and folly, that is not to your credit. It's foolish for you to let somebody beat you black and blue, then turn around and say, 'It's all for Jesus.' That is not submission."

The point I'm trying to make to men is this: don't quote Scripture to a woman unless you are behaving like Jesus does. When you start acting like Jesus, you won't have to demand that your wife submit. When you start loving her like Jesus loves her, when you start forgiving her like Jesus forgives her, when you start blessing her like Jesus blesses her, when you start caring for her and listening to her like Jesus does, she will do anything for you—because she wants a man like Jesus in the house.

A MAN SHOULDN'T QUOTE SCRIPTURE TO A WOMAN UNLESS HE'S BEHAVING LIKE JESUS DOES.

God is saying to men, "Don't you dare demand respect. Don't you dare order submission. Earn it." Remember that Jesus never once commanded anybody to follow Him. Never. He always asked, because He knew who He was and where He was going. He didn't need to demand allegiance to give Himself a sense of importance. And Jesus said, "If you love Me, you'll keep My commandments." Our keeping of His commandments is based on our loving Him. That's the pattern we're to follow in the marriage relationship and really in all relationships between males and females. If a male wants to be a true leader, he must learn who he is in God and become someone who earns respect—someone who loves, guides, and inspires rather than who forces others to do what he wants.

EQUAL AND DIFFERENT

Once men understand the true nature of their strength, what they need to keep in mind is that men and women were created both equal and different. They both have dominion, so that their assignment is the same. However, because men and women have different purposes, designs, and physical bodies, their authority is manifested and carried out in distinct ways.

The male was made first because he was to be responsible for everything and everyone who came after him. God hasn't changed His program. He isn't going to relinquish that responsibility from the male at all. The female that God created needs to understand her purpose as helper.

We aren't to walk around saying, "Well, the culture has changed now. A woman doesn't need to respect a man as the leader in the family." It doesn't matter if the husband is less educated or is making less money than his wife. That does not change God's purpose. The only way to fix our confused society is to get back to God's plan. Purpose, not social change, determines position.

GOD ISN'T GOING TO ABANDON THE MALE'S LEADERSHIP RESPONSIBILITY FOR THE SAKE OF CHANGING CULTURAL ATTITUDES.

A woman can say to her husband, "Let me tell you something. I have a college degree, and you just have your GED. I make more money than you do. I could pay for this house by myself. I don't need you." What kind of spirit is that? I know that some women had that attitude before they were saved and knew God's ways. However, that isn't the perspective we're to have any longer.

I can hear some people saying, "You Christians are always going back to the old days, to the time when men used to walk on women and treat them like doormats." You don't understand what I'm talking about. This is a matter of purpose and position.

Most of us have problems with this concept because we believe that being "different" implies being inferior or superior to others—especially inferior. Don't confuse being different with being lesser. Different does not imply inferiority or superiority; different simply means different. A woman is not less than a man because she is a woman, and a man is not more than a woman because he is a man. Their differences are necessary because of their purposes.

I like the way Paul said it in 1 Corinthians 11:7–8: *"A man...is the image and the glory of God; but the woman is the glory of man. For man did not come from woman, but woman from man."* Is that true? Sure. God caused the man to go into a deep sleep and drew the woman out of him. *"Neither was man created for woman, but woman for man"* (v. 9). Is that true? Yes. God said, *"I will make a helper suitable for him"* (Gen. 2:18).

DIFFERENT DOESN'T IMPLY INFERIORITY OR SUPERIORITY.

"For this reason [purpose], *and because of the angels, the woman ought to have a sign of authority on her head"* (1 Cor. 11:10). The Scripture says, *"For this reason."* In other words, this is God's order in creation, and so men and women should live in that order.

Yet here's what most people forget: *"In the Lord, however, woman is not independent of man, nor is man independent of woman"* (v. 11). God is saying, in effect, "Men and women need one another. They need each other's position." *"For as woman came from man, so also man is born of woman"* (v. 12). I like that. The example Paul used is that men need women to give them birth, but women need men to enable them to conceive. This is definitely not an inferiority-superiority situation. It has to do with purpose. Ephesians 5, which talks about wives submitting to their husbands, also says, *"**Submit to one another** out of reverence for Christ"* (v. 21, emphasis added). There has to be a mutual submitting to one another if God's purposes are to be carried out.

THE RESTORATION OF GOD'S PURPOSE

If men would realize that—

- dominion is not the same thing as domination,

- dominion is to be exercised over the world and not over other people,

114

- submission is something earned rather than demanded,
- men and women are equal but different,
- men and women need one another,

we would go a long way to restoring both harmonious relationships between males and females and God's plan for humanity.

I am convinced that there can be no true dominion over the earth unless God's original design is intact. It is crucial for us to understand the principle that the way we are designed is because of our purpose for existence. The way a male is and the way a female is are directly related to why they exist. They each have been called to special and specific responsibilities in God's kingdom purposes.

In the next three chapters, we'll take a closer look at God's dominion assignments for the male.

PRINCIPLES

1. God created men and women to dominate the earth, not to dominate one another.
2. God's plan is for the individual strengths of men and women to combine to produce exponential results—outcomes much greater than either could accomplish alone.
3. Adam and Eve fell because they stopped looking to their Creator for their purpose and instead looked to themselves. They thought they knew their true purpose better than God did.
4. The results of the Fall were mankind's broken relationship with God and spiritual death, the loss of the balanced relationship between men and women, and the loss of humanity's true dominion over the world.
5. Despite the Fall, God's purposes have never changed. Through the Redeemer, Jesus Christ, these lost and broken relationships and God's dominion purposes can be restored.
6. Men have an innate desire to prove themselves strong, but this has become distorted through sin so that they end up misusing their power and authority.
7. Whenever you abuse your power, you no longer have legitimate authority.
8. Submission is an act of the will of the person submitting. It cannot be forced.
9. A man needs to be a leader by following Jesus' example—by loving, guiding, and inspiring those under his authority, not by demanding that they do what he says.
10. Men and women were created both equal and different.
11. Both men and women have dominion. However, because they have different purposes and designs, their authority is manifested and carried out in distinct ways.
12. A woman is not less than a man because she is a woman, and a man is not more than a woman because he is a man. Their differences are necessary because of their purposes.

6

The Male as Visionary and Leader

G od wants men to understand their dominion assignments and then to develop the qualities that are required in order to carry them out. This is the way that men can pursue God's purpose for their lives and grow in true manhood, for God's purpose is the key to our fulfillment.

The Male as Visionary

The first responsibility that brings fulfillment and spiritual rewards to the male is that of visionary. This is a foundational responsibility because, without it, he can't fulfill the other assignments of leader, teacher, cultivator, protector, and provider.

Being a true visionary is a lost art in our times. The average male can't say who he is because he has no real vision for his life. He is either floundering without purpose, or he is diligently pursuing a false vision based on the values of contemporary society, which are often the opposite of what God values. God wants males to have a vision for their lives that comes from Him and belongs to them personally—not something dictated by the cultural environment, current trends, man-made religion, or someone else's image of what their lives should be.

BEING A TRUE VISIONARY IS A LOST ART TODAY.

WHAT DOES IT MEAN TO HAVE VISION?

In chapter 2, "Seven Principles of Purpose," I asked you to consider several questions, including, "Do you know where you're going? Are you still questioning what you're about?" These are issues related to vision.

Proverbs 29:18 says, *"Where there is no vision, the people perish"* (KJV). Vision is necessary for life. The word *"vision"* in the Hebrew means a "dream, revelation, or oracle." Obviously, a vision that is connected to God's purposes is something that needs to be revealed by God Himself. You need His revelation of your life's vision. The only way you can discover this vision is to listen to what God is saying to you. This is a crucial point that we'll return to shortly.

TO HAVE VISION MEANS TO CONCEIVE OF AND MOVE TOWARD YOUR PURPOSE.

To have vision means to be able to conceive of and move toward your purpose in life. A man shouldn't get married, then say to his wife, "What are we going to do? Well, you know, we'll just wait on the Lord. We'll see where we're going when we get there." That's ridiculous.

Now, it's true that we might not always see the whole picture right away, as Abraham had to trust God to lead him to an unfamiliar land in which he would become a great nation (Gen. 12:1–2). However, Abraham had a clear vision that he was going to the place God had promised him, and he moved steadily toward that goal. Having vision means that you can already see the end of your purpose. It means that you have faith in God and what He has told you to do, so that you are continually moving toward your vision as it is moving toward you. Your responsibility is to support and sustain the vision until it comes to fruition.

CREATED AND DESIGNED FOR VISION

We can know that God has a vision for every male because the male was *created* to be a visionary. Remember that one reason the man was formed first was so that he could be the initial recipient of all the information, revelation, and communication God desired to share regarding humanity's relationship with Him and its purpose for being. Then He created the female to enable the man to fulfill this vision. God's priority has not changed.

When Joel prophesied about the outpouring of the Holy Spirit in the last days, he spoke these words from God: *"I will pour out my Spirit on all people. Your sons and daughters will prophesy, your old men will dream dreams, your young men will see visions"* (Joel 2:28). Notice what this verse says about males. Old men will re-

MALES HAVE BUILT-IN QUALITIES ENABLING THEM TO RECEIVE THE VISION AND TO BRING IT TO PASS.

ceive dreams and young men will see visions from God. It doesn't say that women will see visions. It says that women will prophesy. This means they will speak of the things the men see in the visions. If you look at God's pattern in the Bible, the man is given the vision, but the woman is there to make sure that he accomplishes it. Males and females each have their specific functions.

The male is also *designed* to be a visionary. God created men to be able to look at the big picture in life, to plan for the future from a logical, practical standpoint. Men like to determine what steps are necessary to get from A to B, and all the way to Z. They have built-in qualities that enable them to receive the vision and work to bring it to pass.

PREREQUISITES FOR DISCOVERING VISION

Many men don't have a vision for their lives because they are not committed to God and to seeking His will in this area. If a man does not have relationship with God, he cannot fully function in his purpose.

1. FOLLOW CHRIST'S EXAMPLE

The greatest example of someone who had a vision for His life is Jesus. He constantly repeated and affirmed who He is. Jesus was able to live in the confidence of His purpose from early age. Remember what He said to His parents when He was only twelve years old? *"I must be about*

My Father's business" (Luke 2:49 NKJV). Jesus knew His identity as the Son of God and as God the Son. He said, *"Before Abraham was born, I am!"* (John 8:58). He knew His reason for being and His purpose in life: *"The Son of Man came to seek and to save what was lost"* (Luke 19:10).

The example Jesus set for us by His life shows us our need for these important elements related to purpose: (1) a clear self-image; (2) a life consistent with one's purpose and calling. Jesus lived a life that was totally consistent with who He said He was. He had complete integrity; He always kept and fulfilled His own words.

John the Baptist is another example of a man who knew his identity. He had a sense of confidence in who he was and what he was called to do, so that he could affirm, *"I am the voice of one calling in the desert, 'Make straight the way for the Lord'"* (John 1:23).

The apostle Paul also clearly had a vision for his life. He had a strong self-image and exhibited clarity of purpose. How frequently he began his letters with such statements as, *"Paul, a servant of Christ Jesus, called to be an apostle,"* or *"Paul, an apostle of Christ Jesus by the will of God"* (See, for example, Romans 1:1, Ephesians 1:1.)

WE RECEIVE GOD'S VISION THROUGH OUR ENCOUNTERS WITH HIM.

He also made these statements of purpose: *"For this purpose I was appointed a herald and an apostle"* (1 Tim. 2:7); *"Of this gospel I was appointed a herald and an apostle and a teacher"* (2 Tim. 1:11).

John the Baptist and Paul received God's vision for their lives through their encounters with Him. True vision can be found only in God's presence. Jesus Himself was given to prayer and reflection during His entire earthly life. He was in constant contact with the Father in order to know how to fulfill His life's purpose. After a day of particularly busy ministry in which He had healed the sick and demon-possessed, He got up early the next day and went to pray in a quiet place. When Peter and the other disciples found Him there, they exclaimed, *"Everyone is looking for you!"* (Mark 1:37). Jesus could have basked in the people's praise, but He continued to follow His life's purpose. God had shown Him the next step when He was in prayer. He said, *"Let us go somewhere else—to the nearby villages—so I can preach there also. That is why I have come"* (v. 38).

2. ACKNOWLEDGE CHRIST'S HEADSHIP

The Bible says, *"The head of every man is Christ"* (1 Cor. 11:3). The most important thing a male can do is to acknowledge the headship of Christ and commit to following Him on a daily basis in order to receive His direction. *"I am the way and the truth and the life,"* He said in John 14:6. Ultimately, Jesus Christ not only gives vision, but He *is* the vision, since we are called to be conformed to His image.

3. LISTEN FOR GOD'S DIRECTION

You aren't fulfilling your purpose as a man until you can hear the voice of God. You aren't fulfilling your purpose as a man until you start speaking and affirming the Word of God in your life. To do this, you need to be in the same garden environment that Adam was first placed in.

We need to get back to the place where the glory can flow between God and man, where we can hear the voice of God, and God can give us direction. Because the Holy Spirit has been poured out into the hearts of believers, the garden is no longer just one spot on the earth—it is within the heart of every man who belongs to Christ. That is why Christ said, *"The kingdom of God is within you"* (Luke 17:21). It is not within you of its own accord; the kingdom of God is within you because God Spirit lives within you.

The kingdom of God—God's Spirit and will ruling in our hearts—has come to us through Christ, and it is through Him that we can fulfill the dominion mandate. We are called to spread the gospel message of reconciliation with God through Christ and of the gift of the Holy Spirit—who brings us power for living, working, and creating to the glory of God. If we want to fulfill our dominion responsibilities and assignments, we have to do so through the Spirit of Christ as we follow God's will.

I believe that many men think, "It's the preacher's job to stay in the presence of the Lord." Yet men are to function as priests in their homes. One of the things that blesses me about Abraham is that he would go to his wife and say, "The Lord says so-and-so." Men need to stay close to God so they can tell their families what God is saying to them. Many men can tell their families what the Dow-Jones average is or what the status of the local economy is. But they need to be able to tell them, "This is what God says is important." Women need somebody who can tell them what God is saying. Many women go from prayer meeting to prayer meeting and to this or that prophetess because there isn't a man in the house providing them with vision.

MEN ARE TO FUNCTION AS PRIESTS IN THEIR HOMES.

In other words, you shouldn't depend on the preacher to lead your family. Don't go to church and say, "Well, preacher, tell me what to do." You had better find out from God what to do for your own family. The presence of the Lord is key.

4. BE OPEN TO GOD'S COMMUNICATION

God can communicate vision in a variety of ways. First, He speaks as we pray and read His Word. These are among the most important habits we can develop. God may also speak through the counsel of trusted Christians, or as we conduct an assessment of our gifts and talents. Is there one idea or vocation that keeps coming to your mind, especially after prayer? That may well be God's vision for your life. You should also allow God to broaden and expand a vision He has already given you. Remember that when we've been faithful in smaller things, He often promotes us to larger ones. A vision may also be inherited, but the man who inherits it needs to make it his own and exercise true leadership in fulfilling that vision.

"WHERE THERE IS NO VISION"

A man needs a clear vision of these three things: (1) who he is in God, (2) what his overall purpose as a male is, and

122

(3) what his purpose as an individual man is. In this way, he can know where he is going in life and can lead those under his care and responsibility.

First things have to come first. Before God gave the man a helper, He gave him a vision for what he should be doing. That is also the order we need to follow today.

If a man has no vision, or if his wife has the only vision, the man and his whole family will have a difficult time. This is because God has designed the male to carry others with him in his vision. Our society is in trouble because wherever the man goes, he brings everybody else along. Right now, most men don't know where they're going, and the women and children who are following have no direction.

It's dangerous for a woman to marry a man who doesn't know God, because she won't know where he's taking her. Even if he does know God, he needs to learn to live in God's presence, because some men who know Him don't talk to Him enough. No man has the right to lead a woman if he doesn't have the ability to truly hear God. *"Where there is no vision, the people perish"* (Prov. 29:18 KJV).

This is a serious matter. It means that a male-man cannot ask a female-man to follow and help him if he isn't really doing anything. Where is she supposed to be going? What is she supposed to help him with? The woman is looking for somebody who is doing something to which she can contribute. All the potential, all the energy, all the excitement, and all the creativity within her has to be applied to something. There are many women who have skills and abilities, but men aren't doing anything they can help with. Some women wait for weeks, months, even years with latent skills, eager to help fathers, husbands, friends, employers—to no avail. The resulting lack of direction can sometimes make women vulnerable to making mistakes. A woman needs to have direction and be involved in meaningful activity in order to fulfill her purpose.

BEFORE GOD GAVE THE MAN A HELPER, HE GAVE HIM A VISION.

Remember that the man wasn't meant to fulfill the vision himself. God created the woman to enable the man to accomplish the purpose for which they were both created. Everything the woman has was made to help the male. All her abilities were designed for his vision. Therefore, the woman's purpose cannot be truly fulfilled without the man's purpose—and vice versa. God has special plans for each woman's gifts and talents. Yet because of the way he designed humanity, a woman needs a man who has vision in order for all her purposes to be fulfilled. This applies not only to marriage but also to the church and to the workplace. Ministers, employers, and others in leadership positions need to provide vision for those whom they are leading. Otherwise, the things they and their followers are involved in doing will lack meaning and be unfulfilling.

VISION IS MORE IMPORTANT THAN MONEY OR EVEN DISCIPLINE.

When a man has no vision, he causes a woman to feel insecure. One of the saddest things a husband can do is to sit down with his wife and say, "What should we do?" That sounds very nice and democratic. However, because it is the man's responsibility to provide vision, his having a goal and direction in life brings her a needed sense of security.

Vision is therefore more important than money. A man may have a large amount of money, but no vision beyond accruing wealth or indulging in wild speculation. He might have hit pay dirt in some deal, but this doesn't mean he has vision. Many wealthy people don't have real purpose in life.

Men need vision even before discipline, because discipline comes from vision. Discipline comes as you plan ahead and make sacrifices to fulfill your vision.

GOD ALWAYS PROVIDES FOR THE VISION

How do you know your vision will come to fruition? Rest assured that God always provides for the vision He gives us. The Garden was God's provision to enable Adam to carry out the dominion purpose He had given him. God will always support and sustain His own vision. That is

His responsibility. But the man has to seek and receive the vision in order to secure the provision.

THE MALE AS LEADER

After the male has secured a vision, he is ready for leadership. Most of us have developed our images of what it means to be a leader from the wrong sources, so we need to rethink this concept. We have looked to movie stars, famous sports figures, singers, and politicians as our role models. Yet the majority of famous men don't know what a true man is. If you don't believe me, ask them where their children are. Ask them where their wives are. Ask them how their home life is. The majority of the wealthiest, most **WE HAVE DEVELOPED OUR IMAGES OF LEADERSHIP FROM THE WRONG SOURCES.** famous, most prestigious men in the world can't keep their homes together. Our problem is that we have looked to status and personal accomplishment as the measure of manhood rather than to God's standards. He is concerned with men who have a vision from Him and who can support, sustain, and nurture their families and others as they move toward this vision in pursuit of God and His purposes.

CREATED AND DESIGNED TO LEAD

I've found that some men want to run away from the responsibility of leadership. They look at it as too much of a burden. They let their wives run everything. Others want to selfishly pursue their own interests without worrying about the needs of others. Certain men don't think they deserve to be leaders. They think you have to be rich or highly educated in order to lead.

One time, when I was speaking in Pittsburgh, I chatted with a young lady who was vice president of a bank, twenty-eight years old, and unmarried. She said to me, "I just wish that God would bless me with someone like you. You know, I really have everything I need: I have my own condominium, I make over $50,000 a year, and I could have bought a Porsche. But I decided that I wouldn't buy a Porsche because it would intimidate men. It would give the wrong signal. I bought a lesser car so that I would not frighten them away."

I said to her, "You have the wrong idea. You shouldn't marry any man who would be intimidated by a Porsche, because that would mean the man is insecure. It would mean that the man equates his position with what he owns. When insecurity marries insecurity, you're going to have problems all your life."

If you are the president of a company, it doesn't matter if your secretary drives a Jaguar. You are still the president. As a man, you can't allow your self-image to be dependent upon what someone else has. God made you the head, and if you meet a woman with a Porsche, who is the vice president of a bank and has her own real estate assets, there is nothing wrong with that. What are you scared of? You need to understand that that kind of woman is a blessing. And if you give her leadership, she'll be glad to share her assets. She just wants to know that you will handle them well.

IF YOU ARE A MALE, YOU WERE BORN TO LEAD.

Let me make something very clear: if you are a male, you were born to lead. God made the male first because He wanted him to be responsible. A male doesn't decide to lead or not to lead. He has his position by virtue of his purpose. The male is not the head of his home because he has to lead. He has to lead because he *is* the head. His position is inherent. No male can sit down and debate whether he will lead his home, whether he will go to work for his family. That is not a debatable issue.

The male was designed for *responsible* leadership. He is to lead and be responsible for everything under his jurisdiction. (God may use women in leadership, also, but this is one of the primary purposes of the male. For more on women in leadership, please refer to my book *Understanding the Purpose and Power of Woman.*)

God both *created* and *designed* the male to be a leader. Remember the principle? You are the way you are because of why you are. Therefore, the male already has leadership qualities within him. However, he needs to rediscover the characteristics of leadership so that he can work on developing his God-given qualities and become an effective leader.

CHARACTERISTICS OF A LEADER

1. STRONG AND COURAGEOUS

The male has been designed to take risks and meet challenges. God often gives men assignments that seem too big for them—and they are. They can be accomplished only through God's help. Yet the qualities of courage, strength, and daring enable men to take the necessary steps of faith that bring God's intervention.

The Lord said to Joshua, *"Be strong and courageous, because you will lead"* (Josh. 1:6). It's impossible to be the leader of the family and of society if you are not strong and courageous. And Joshua had a family of three million people! God gave this young Israelite a job designed for a man.

2. OBEDIENT TO GOD'S COMMANDS

God added something to His command to Joshua. He said, "Be careful to obey all the commands." (See verse 7.) A strong man has to be submitted to God's authority. No man can be strong if he is not accountable to someone else. A real man doesn't ignore authority. He remains in the garden of God's presence, praying and reading God's Word, so that he may understand and obey His commands.

Some men take their courage and strength and use them recklessly. When a man turns from God, takes his life into his own hands, and doesn't combine courage with common sense, he can cause himself and his family many problems. True courage and strength come only through confidence in the faithfulness of God and belief in His Word.

3. A LOGICAL THINKER

To be a leader, you have to be a logical thinker and keep a clear mind. You have to identity what the specific problems are, analyze them, calculate what needs to be done to solve them, make a decision (sometimes very quickly), and act on it. You cannot be affected by your environment to the point where it immobilizes you, and your feelings rule you. You cannot be controlled by your emotions.

Now, while a male has emotions, he is not guided by them the way a woman often is. A woman has been made by God to integrate her emotions into everything she sees and thinks. This is not a negative trait, but rather God's built-in gift that enables her to empathize with others and to bring God's compassion and mercy to situations.

A leader often cannot be ruled by emotion or sentiment, especially when he has to make difficult decisions. That is why God designed a male differently **A MALE HAS** from a female. The male is not emo-**EMOTIONS, BUT** tional, even though he has emotions. **IS NOT RULED** He feels a great deal, but because of **BY THEM.** his purpose, his feelings are generally not his principle consideration. He's led by his thinking. Because of this trait, women can get the impression that men are cold. They're not cold; they're just not influenced as much by their emotions.

Think of Moses and the Israelites standing on the outskirts of the Red Sea with Pharaoh and his army approaching to destroy them. I can imagine Moses' sister, Miriam, having an emotional reaction and saying, "Ahhhh! God, do something!" But Moses is coolheaded. The Bible says Moses stood up and said, *"The LORD will fight for you, and you shall hold your peace"* (Exod. 14:14 NKJV). He was essentially saying, "Be at peace; I promise you'll be all right," while at the same time Pharaoh was coming after them with thousands of his soldiers.

The Israelites had no way of escape: the sea was in front of them; the Egyptians were behind them. Yet in the midst of this situation, we see this cool, collected, calm male. His calmness caused all the Israelites to quiet down, also. They knew Moses had never lied before. When he said something, it happened.

I can see Moses, after he'd finished speaking, standing behind a bush and crying to the Lord, "Did you hear what I told them? O God, please help...." God said to Moses, *"Why are you crying out to me? Tell the Israelites to move on"* (v. 15). I guess what the Word of God is trying to teach us is that a leader is somebody who never transfers his fear to those for whom he's responsible. I didn't say he never has fear—but he doesn't let his fear infect others.

4. A SERVANT'S HEART

A real man, a true leader, is a servant. He is not a ruler. He takes care of others before himself. Jesus said,

> *You know that the rulers of the Gentiles lord it over them, and their high officials exercise authority over them. Not so with you. Instead, whoever wants to become great among you must be your servant, and whoever wants to be first must be your slave—just as the Son of Man did not come to be served, but to serve, and to give his life as a ransom for many.* (Matt. 20:25–28)

The apostle Paul echoed this theme when he wrote, *"Each of you should look not only to your own interests, but also to the interests of others"* (Phil. 2:4), and *"Husbands, love your wives, just as Christ loved the church and gave himself up for her"* (Eph. 5:25). How did Christ love His church? First of all, by giving Himself for her. This means that a man should give up his personal, private, ambitious, egotistical desires in order to serve his wife and family. He needs to emulate Christ's nature.

5. A TEACHABLE SPIRIT

A true leader has humility, so that he is willing to learn from others and be corrected, when need be. Some of the greatest moments in my life are times when my wife corrects me, gives me ideas, or provides insight on something that I haven't been able to do right. My wife has awesome resources within her. It takes a real man to submit to help. It takes a fool to avoid it. God is not looking for a controller. He is looking for a leader who makes himself fruitful by being pruned when necessary in order to yield a healthier and greater harvest.

Men need to remember that women are here to help them. I believe that one of the reasons God took the woman from the man's side, or rib, is to emphasize her nature. The word *rib* means "sustainer" or "supporter." That's what the rib does. It supports the whole upper frame with the vertebrae. So a woman is a support system. If she functions in her purpose, she helps the male to function in his.

WHAT A WOMAN CAN DO

I would like to say a special word here to the women reading this book. God said it wasn't good for the man to be alone, so He created the woman. You are good for a man. One of the ways you can be good to him is to show him respect as the leader in the home.

Sometimes a husband will say, "I think we should do this," and right away his wife will show him she doesn't trust him. She'll say, "Do *what?* You've never done anything right yet!" She just wiped out the man's ego. What she can say if she isn't sure about his idea is, "Well, let's try it that way, then." When she says, "try," he hears "trust." "Let's try it" means she's going to trust him in this undertaking. Then, if he messes up, she can say, "We all mess up." A woman can protect her husband's face, realizing that she also makes mistakes.

Feed your husband's need for leadership respect. No matter what he does, just keep feeding it. When you get it to the point where it is strong and effective, then it will become a great blessing to both of you. He will learn to lead because he will know that you support him.

A STRONG FOUNDATION

Learning to become both a visionary and a leader is crucial for the male because it enables him to have a strong foundation for fulfilling his other dominion assignments. In the next chapter, we'll look at two more of these responsibilities: teacher and cultivator.

PRINCIPLES

1. Being a visionary is a foundational responsibility for the male because, without it, he can't fulfill his other assignments of leader, teacher, cultivator, provider, and protector.

2. To have vision means to be able to conceive of and move toward your purpose in life.

3. The male was *created* to be a visionary. He was given the first vision of God's plan for humanity.

4. The male is *designed* to be a visionary. He is able to look at the big picture in life and to plan for the future from a logical, practical standpoint.

5. Prerequisites for discovering vision are: (1) follow Christ's example, (2) acknowledge Christ's headship, (3) listen for God's direction, and (4) be open to God's communication.

6. A man needs a clear vision of (1) who he is in God, (2) what his overall purpose as a male is, (3) what his purpose as an individual man is.

7. God designed the male to carry others with him in his vision.

8. If a man has no vision, this will negatively affect those who are to follow him, especially his family.

9. Before God gave the man a helper, He gave him a vision.

10. A male cannot ask a female to follow and help him if he has no vision.

11. God always provides for the vision He gives.

12. God created and designed the male to be a responsible leader.

13. The characteristics of a leader are: (1) strong and courageous, (2) obedient to God's commands, (3) a logical thinker, (4) a servant's heart, and (5) a teachable spirit.

14. One way a woman can be good to a man is by respecting him as the leader in the home.

7

THE MALE AS TEACHER AND CULTIVATOR

WHEN A MAN TEACHES HIS FAMILY GOD'S WORD AND WAYS, HE ATTRACTS GOD'S TRUST AND FRIENDSHIP.

The dominion assignments of teacher and cultivator are an integral part of God's purpose and design for the male. The importance of men's involvement in teaching God's Word to the members of their families and others within their realms of influence and of encouraging them in their personal growth needs to be recaptured today.

THE MALE AS TEACHER

We've seen that God gave Adam specific instructions regarding how mankind should live and work in the Garden, and that He left it up to Adam to communicate to Eve what he had been told. In this way, God set the precedent for the male to be the primary teacher of the family.

Some men believe that because they have a responsibility to teach, they are more intelligent than women. If this were a matter of intelligence, many women would blow us away, men! Being a teacher doesn't mean that you are more intelligent—it simply means that your purpose is to communicate God's Word and will to your family.

CREATED TO TEACH

The male was *created* to be the spiritual leader and teacher of his family. The Bible says that if a wife has a question about a spiritual matter during church, she should ask her husband about it when they get home. (See 1 Corinthians 14:35.) Why? He is supposed to know the Word. Yet most women know more of the Word than men do. How can a man be a teacher if he doesn't know the lessons?

Ephesians 6:4 says, *"Fathers, do not exasperate your children; instead, bring them up in the training and instruction of the Lord."* Too often, fathers leave this responsibility solely to the mothers. This becomes especially difficult for women when the children reach a certain age in which they don't want to submit to authority. Men need to set a strong spiritual example for their children, especially at that particular time in their lives.

MEN NEED TO SET A STRONG SPIRITUAL EXAMPLE FOR THEIR FAMILIES.

DESIGNED TO TEACH

As was the case with the male's responsibilities as visionary and leader, the man has been *designed* with the capacity to fulfill his purpose of teaching.

Teaching is in the nature of a man. A teacher is always going to tell you how to do something. Sometimes it appears to women as if men are telling them what to do all the time. Suppose a husband comes home from work and notices that the kitchen is in disarray. He tells his wife there's a more efficient way to organize it and is surprised when she says, "Who do you think you are? I've been slaving in the house cleaning and taking care of the children all day, and now you want to tell me how to organize my kitchen?" But this is his nature. I'm talking about the teaching tendency of a man now, not necessarily how he should communicate his information.

Why does a man always want to correct things? A teacher desires to give input. He wants to feel as if he is responsible for the progress of his "class." Therefore, he gives instructions, advice, and counsel. Now, his advice might not be any good, but he still wants to give it. What his wife can do in this particular circumstance is to nod and say, with sincerity, "Thank you for your suggestion" and then go and do what she thinks is best. He often just needs to feel as if he's listened to and that his suggestions are appreciated.

One of the best things a woman can say to a man is, "Tell me more." Encourage him. When you reject his teaching gift, you're frustrating his very nature. What he needs is to have this teaching quality built up in him. This is part of what a wife can do to show respect to her husband.

TEACHING ATTRACTS THE TRUST OF GOD

Abraham was the first man that God called His friend (Isa. 41:8). Why did God like Abraham? We find out in Genesis 18. In verses 20–21 God indicated that He was going to destroy Sodom and Gomorrah for their wickedness. Yet just before this, He said, *"Shall I hide from Abraham what I am about to do?"* (v. 17). He continued,

> *Abraham will surely become a great and powerful nation, and all nations on earth will be blessed through him. For I have chosen him* ["know him" KJV], *so that he will direct his children and his household after him to keep the way of the LORD by doing what is right and just, so that the LORD will bring about for Abraham what he has promised him.* (vv. 18–19)

God liked Abraham for the same reason He chose Him: He knew his character. What did He know about Abraham? *"He will direct his children and his household after him to keep the way of the LORD by doing what is right and just."*

God was saying, "I like Abraham because I can trust him. I know I can trust him because his home is in order. I won't keep any secrets from him." God didn't say He liked Abraham because he spoke in tongues or worked miracles or even because he prayed. He didn't say He liked Abraham because he was a famous preacher, teacher, or evangelist. He said, "I like Abraham because he will teach his wife, his family, his entire household the Word of God."

KNOWING THE WORD

If a man doesn't have the knowledge and the capability to teach a woman the Word of God, then he is not really ready for marriage. Getting past puberty doesn't make you ready for marriage. Getting a job or college degree doesn't make you ready. I'm talking about God's qualifications. As far as God is concerned, you are ready for marriage when you are able to teach your family His Word. If you are already married but don't know the Word, you should make it a priority to study and gain knowledge of the Bible. You should go to a church where you can learn the Scriptures, so you can follow up on what God has commanded you to do as a man. You can't teach what you don't know.

IF A MAN CAN'T TEACH THE WORD, HE'S NOT READY FOR MARRIAGE.

How can you teach the Word of God to your family if all you watch is television sitcoms or *Survivor* or ball games? How can you teach your family the Word of God if all you read is *Superman* and *Fantastic Four* or *Time* and *Newsweek*? How can you teach the Word of God to your family if you haven't spent any time learning it yourself?

There are men who know more about sports than the Bible. They can name every baseball team, who plays on them, and who is pitching in the series, but they don't know the Word of God. They can instruct their boys in how to play soccer, but they don't know how to teach them to be sanctified.

Someone may say, "The Bible is one thing, but I'm teaching my boy how to be a *real* man." What are you teaching him? A young man told me how his father said to him one day, "Come, I want to show you how to be a man." His father took him to his favorite poolside club, sat him on a stool, and told the waitress, "Give this man a heavy drink. It's time for him to become a man now. He's sixteen." He told his son, "Now, if you can hold your liquor, you're a real man." And while they were sitting there, he pointed out a nearly naked girl at the pool. He said, "You see that girl? A real man knows how to handle her." This was a son being taught by his father how to be a man.

Some men think they're teaching their boys how to be men by taking them to ball games to watch men fight over a pigskin. They say, "That's a man. A man knocks people down and beats them half to death on a ball field." You don't instruct your son in what it means to be a real man by teaching him how to drink or play ball. It takes a man to teach a boy the Word of God, to instruct him in the values and principles of life that will live on after the game is over.

Abraham was a man who took his responsibility as the head of the home seriously. And the Lord said, "I know Abraham." I wonder—does God know you? Can He say about you, "I know that you will teach your family the Word of God"?

If you want God to consider you His friend, then become a teacher in your home. You have to be full of the Word in order to give it to your family. There are many, many men who still don't understand and appreciate the value of the Word of God for the fulfillment of their purpose.

Many men just drop their wives off at church and send their children to Sunday school because they don't want to be responsible for their spiritual training. Abraham knew the Word, and he taught it. And God said, "I will not hide anything from Abraham." Wouldn't you like to be the kind of man to whom God says, "I'm going to tell you My secrets"?

A man who instructs his household in the Scriptures attracts God. No matter how much you pray and go to church and sing hymns, if you don't teach your household God's ways, if you don't give the Word of God prominence in your home by making it your guide for living, then God sees you as a weak man.

DOES GOD KNOW YOU? Do you know there are preachers who can preach you out of your seat, but who can't sit civilly with their wives at the dinner table? God is not interested in their preaching as much as in how they conduct themselves in their homes. Some people teach great theological discourses, and they can impress you with their head knowledge. But God says in 1 Timothy 3, in effect, "Look, if a man wants to be a leader in the church, first let him get his house in order." (See verse 12.)

God doesn't measure your ability to lead by your religious or academic qualifications. He measures it by your domestic qualifications. If you can take care of your children, then God says, "All right, now you can lead My church." If you can manage your home, then you can manage the house of God.

HOW TO TEACH THE WORD TO YOUR FAMILY

In Deuteronomy 4, Moses gave instructions from God to heads of households about specific ways in which they were to teach their families His Word. First, he said,

> *Be careful, and watch yourselves closely so that you do not forget the things your eyes have seen or let them slip from your heart as long as you live. Teach them to your children and to their children after them.* (v. 9)

God is saying to men, "Don't let My ways out of your sight. Make sure you understand and obey them first. Then *"teach them to your children and to their children after them."* Why? Because you are supposed to be the teacher.

Don't just tell your children, "Do this," or "Don't do that." Show them. Watch your life and make sure you keep the Word of God. Some men say one thing but do another. For example, they may tell their children to be honest but then call off work when they're not sick. Some fathers tell their children, "Tobacco is bad for you," while at the same time they're puffing away on a cigarette. Do you know what **SOME MEN SAY ONE THING BUT DO ANOTHER.** children see when they see adults smoking? They see an adult world, and they say, "To be a grown-up, you have to smoke." Adults reinforce this idea by their actions.

God tells us not to do this to our children. People don't seem to understand that you cannot teach something if you're not being an example of it yourself. A good teacher is one who teaches by example.

"Teach them to your children and to their children after them." I want to say a word here to grandparents. When your daughter or son sends that little boy to you, what does he go back home with? Some kids learn things from their

grandparents that are disgraceful. Parents find their little children coming back home cursing or telling foul stories, and they wonder where they are hearing them. They're getting them from Grandpa and Grandma! Your children's children should get the Word from you. When your children send their kids to you, those kids should go back home knowing more about God.

God is very concerned that parents teach their children. He isn't saying here to send your children to church, Sunday school, or vacation Bible club. He's saying to teach them yourself. These other things are good, but if they're not reinforced in the home, children can get the impression their parents don't think the Bible is important. Parents don't realize the negative impact this attitude can have on their families.

After giving God's commands to the people, Moses said,

These commandments that I give you today are to be upon your hearts. Impress them on your children. Talk about them when you sit at home and when you walk along the road, when you lie down and when you get up. Tie them as symbols on your hands and bind them on your foreheads. Write them on the doorframes of your houses and on your gates. (Deut. 6:6–9)

First of all, God says, *"Impress* [My commandments] *on your children."* Then He tells how to do it.

1. "TALK ABOUT THEM WHEN YOU SIT AT HOME."

What do your children hear in your house? What do they hear when you sit down to eat? Some scandal reported in the newspaper? The latest movie? What do you discuss? Do you talk about the goodness of the Lord? When you sit around your house during your leisure time, what do you do? Do you spend time teaching your children the Word? Do you have family devotions?

2. "TALK ABOUT THEM...WHEN YOU WALK ALONG THE ROAD."

What do you talk about when you drive your children to school or go on outings and trips? Do you yell at other drivers, or listen to less-than-edifying radio shows? What example do you set for your children when you're out in public? Do you talk about others behind their backs? Or do you live out God's Word in a natural, everyday way?

Some men never talk about God outside the church. It hurts me when I see men ashamed of the Gospel of Jesus Christ. They think they're supposed to be cool, and to be cool, they can't talk about Jesus. God says, "A real man that I respect is a man who won't just have devotions at home, but will walk out into the world and talk about Me along the 'road'—where he works, shops, and rec-reates."

> **DO YOU LIVE OUT GOD'S WORD IN A NATURAL, EVERYDAY WAY?**

When you go to work, you don't just hide your Christi-anity under your paperwork. You tell people about Jesus right there on the job. Right there on the street. Don't be ashamed to tell them about the One who died for you.

3. "TALK ABOUT THEM...WHEN YOU LIE DOWN."

Before you say goodnight to your children or tuck them into bed, what words do you leave them with? The assurance of God's presence and peace during the night? An encour-aging psalm? Or do you wave them off to bed while you fin-ish working on something?

What do you think about before you drift off to sleep? Do you know that the last thing you think about at night is usually the first thing you think about when you wake up? Sometimes you dream about it. It amazes me that people de-liberately think about the worst things. Some of you read the worst kind of books before you go to bed. Then you wonder why your spirit is disturbed.

4. "TALK ABOUT THEM...WHEN YOU GET UP."

When you wake up in the morning, you will more likely think about the Word of God if you have meditated on it before going to bed. And you will start ministering as you talk about it with your family.

How do you usually greet your children in the morning? With a quiet reminder of God's love and strength for the day? What spiritual armor do you send them off to school with? It's a difficult world for children to grow up in today, and they need God's Word to fortify them.

5. "TIE THEM AS SYMBOLS ON YOUR HANDS AND BIND THEM ON YOUR FOREHEADS. WRITE THEM ON THE DOOR-FRAMES OF YOUR HOUSES AND ON YOUR GATES."

The point God is trying to make in the above passage is that whatever your hands find to do, make sure it is in accordance with the Word. Whatever is in your thoughts, make sure it's the Word of God. *"The doorframes"*—I like that. The doorposts in Moses' day were two major posts that held up the frame of the house. Anyone who came through those doorposts came into your home. This means that all of your house should be held up by the Word of God, and that you are supposed to check who comes into your house to make sure they pass through the Word of God.

God is saying to fathers and young men who aspire to be good fathers, "Get the Word in you. Plaster your whole life with the Word." If anybody wants access to your life or your home, he is to come through the Word of God. If any woman wants to marry you, tell her straight, "If you don't know God and His Word, I don't care how cute you look or how much you can give me—forget it."

I would love for God to raise up men who wouldn't compromise, who wouldn't marry a woman who's not a woman of God. Sometimes we don't have any standards. We have to have standards and values again. Our values come from what we believe. They create our morals and affect our behavior. If we believe the Word of God, that's our value system.

THE MALE AS CULTIVATOR

Knowing the Word of God is also essential for men if they are to fulfill their responsibility as cultivators of the spiritual and personal lives of their family members.

140

THE MALE AS TEACHER AND CULTIVATOR

CREATED AND DESIGNED TO CULTIVATE

Before Eve was created, God placed Adam in the Garden and told him to cultivate it. (See Genesis 2:15 NAS.) To cultivate means to make something better than when you first received it. If a male receives something to work with, he should never end up with just what he was given. When he's finished working with it, it should be multiplied, more effective, more fruitful. God told the man to be a developer, and any male who wants to be a real man will appreciate his responsibility to make everything around him better.

Some men concentrate on only their own fruit, their own accomplishments. They are just bettering themselves. That's called selfishness. They don't have fruitful wives or children because they've neglected to care for them. A real man looks out for the needs of others and helps them to grow.

1. CULTIVATOR OF HIS WORK, TALENTS, AND SKILLS

First, a male has been designed to do his work in such a way that he is able to make it into more than it was originally. In the parable of the talents, the man traveling out of the country entrusted the first servant with five talents, the second with two, and the third with one. It is implied that the man said to them, "Now, when I come back, I don't want to see just the money I gave you. I want to see an increase in my investment." When the man returned, and the servant with the one talent had done nothing to increase his master's money, he was called *"wicked"* and *"lazy"* (Matt. 25:26). If a man is still working at what he was working at ten years ago and hasn't improved it at all, there's something wrong.

> **TO CULTIVATE MEANS TO MULTIPLY, MAKE FRUITFUL, MAKE BETTER.**

Every part of society should be developing if we have real men in our presence. But too often we have destroyers instead of developers. They are tearing down our homes, spraying graffiti on our buildings, stealing, and shooting. Male-men need to come back to their purpose and stop using their strength for the wrong reasons.

2. CULTIVATOR OF HIS CHILDREN

A man is also meant to cultivate his children, to provide an environment for their personal and spiritual growth. Again, he can do this only if he is saturated with the Word.

Fathers should build up rather than tear down. For instance, you should never tell your children that they are stupid. Why? Those children are your seed. You need to nurture them so they will grow and blossom. Remember, the chip comes from the old block, so the block shouldn't criticize it. When your children do something wrong, you should firmly but gently correct them.

A FATHER SHOULD HELP HIS CHILDREN TO DISCOVER THEIR GIFTS.

A father should help his children to discover their gifts and talents. He should affirm their accomplishments and tell them what they can become in life, so they can have a positive outlook based on faith in God. Children need to be encouraged. I will talk more about this topic in the chapter, "How to Be a Good Father."

3. CULTIVATOR OF HIS WIFE

Men have a special responsibility for cultivating their wives. Yet because they often have unrealistic ideas about women, they can end up neglecting or hurting them.

Most of us men are walking around with specific pictures in our minds of who we want our wives to be, and when they don't meet our expectations, we tend to blame them. At one point, God showed me that I had this attitude toward my wife, and He had to correct me.

Here's the way a man often thinks: he is a certain type of man, so he wants a certain type of woman. He thinks such things as: "I am a musician, so I want her to sing." "I'm a banker, so I want her to know about finance." "I am slim, so I want her to be slim." "I want her to be smart." "I want a woman who dresses well." "I like long hair on a woman." Now, there isn't anything wrong with desiring these things. However, I want to tell you something: *the "perfect" woman you are looking for does not exist.*

It is your job to cultivate your wife so that she can be all that God created her to be. You are to help her to blossom and grow into God's woman, not tear her down because she doesn't meet your specifications. In addition, you can help your wife become all that you saw in her when you first met her, and which you now think is missing. You need to nurture all the potential she has. This is not to be done in a controlling way, but in a loving and giving way, which is the nature of Christ. Perhaps it is your criticism that is preventing her from being the woman you want her to be. Think about it: what pressures are present in her life that are keeping her from being all that she desires and needs to be?

> **A MAN IS TO CULTIVATE HIS WIFE SO SHE CAN BE ALL GOD CREATED HER TO BE.**

Let me say a word here to the young, unmarried men: what are you cultivating? When a young lady comes into your presence, she should leave a better person than she came. She may try to come on too strong, vulgar, like a prostitute. Yet when she leaves, she should walk away a lady. If someone asks her, "What happened to you?" she should be able to say, "I met a man who told me he wouldn't sleep with me. He wouldn't degrade me. Why? Because he respects me." Cultivate these young ladies. Don't drag them down, and don't let them drag you down. A young woman shouldn't leave your presence pregnant. She should leave with her dignity and her virginity. Give these young women some good soil. Give them something to make them better. That's being a real man.

HOW TO CULTIVATE YOUR WIFE

If you are a man, God has created and designed you to cultivate anything you desire, including your family. So whenever a man receives a woman as a wife, he is given the opportunity to exercise his cultivation ability. A man should pray and ask God to show him how to cultivate his wife. He is to water her, prune her, and give her sunlight. He is to add nutrients to her life until she blossoms into the woman she is meant to be.

Now, God designed the male to be able to cultivate and produce a beautiful tree. Therefore, if the tree looks like an old bush after twelve years, it's not the woman's fault. The cultivator was not putting in the right nutrients and the right water. A woman should be flourishing under her husband's loving care. Men, don't go looking for someone else whom you believe is more like what you want your wife to be. You are the cultivator—cultivate your wife.

For example, if you want her to look nice, buy some nice clothes for her. Let her go to the beauty salon. Stop telling her to look good if you're going to refuse to pay for a hairdresser. Stop telling her you want her to look slim when you ask her to serve fatty foods. Tell her you want to exercise together. Don't just wish for something and then not cultivate it. Leaders don't point the way; they lead the way.

Some women have been living with men who are pouring acid on their roots and drying up their fruit. Men, it's difficult for you to cultivate if you have poison on your hands. You shouldn't try to transplant a tender plant to your garden if you have acid in your soil. Make sure you have good soil before you try to cultivate.

Cultivate your wife by sending her roses. Bring her nutrients by calling her up and saying, "Honey, I love you." Give her sunlight by telling her she's beautiful.

WHEN A MAN FINISHES CULTIVATING, HE SHOULD HAVE SOMETHING TO PRESENT.

Ephesians 5:25–26 says that Jesus loved His bride and gave His life for her. He washed her with water through the Word. Verse 27 says that He did this so that He may *"present her."* This means that when a man is finished cultivating, he should have something to present. "Lord, see how I cultivated my wife? We've been married only five years. Wait until You see the next fifteen."

At the end of your life, your wife should be so close to what you first saw when you desired her that you can die with peace. You should be proud of the woman that you cultivated. Jesus presents His wife, saying, "Look what I have!" The woman described in Proverbs 31 is amazing.

"Her husband has full confidence in her and lacks nothing of value" (v. 11). *"Her husband is respected at the city gate, where he takes his seat among the elders of the land"* (v. 23). If anyone passed by this husband, he said proudly, "Do you see that woman? That's my lady over there." Many husbands haven't done anything for their wives. Instead of cultivating, they have taken soil away from them. Now that their wives have become run down both emotionally and physically, they are ashamed to be seen with them.

Are you ashamed to bring people to your house? Instead, you should be ashamed of yourself. And guess what? You *are* ashamed of yourself. According to the Word, your wife is your own flesh. (See Ephesians 5:28.) Whatever she looks like is really a sign of what you look like.

Now, a man doesn't always know what to do to cultivate his wife. A woman can help her husband in this. She can let him know what she needs so he can provide the right nutrients. For instance, if he says, "Honey, you seem upset today. What happened?" she can say, "Well, I've been trying to work with these old pots and pans. Every time I pick them up the handles fall off, and it's frustrating. If we bought some new pots, it would make meal preparation much less stressful for me." Or if he says, "I want to be able to talk to you about my job, but you can't seem to discuss it," she can say, "Well, sweetheart, sit down and tell me about it. I want to know about your job. Teach me."

How is she going to converse with you about your job if you don't talk to her about it, if you don't come home and tell her what you're doing, what you're planning, and how your job works? You talk to the young lady at the office. She knows about your job, so you think she's better than your wife. She isn't better than your wife. Your wife is better than you are. You are the one who is lacking understanding, because you didn't take the time to teach her.

WASHING WITH THE WORD

Husbands, love your wives, just as Christ loved the church and gave himself up for her to make her holy, cleansing her by the washing with water through the word, and to present her to himself as a radiant church, without stain or wrinkle or any other blemish, but holy and blameless. In this same way, husbands ought to love their wives as their own bodies. He who loves his wife loves himself. (Eph. 5:25–28)

In this passage, Paul was saying, "Jesus is a good Husband. A man ought to love his wife like Jesus loved the church. He gave Himself for her and cleansed her by the washing of water through the Word. Why? In order *"to present her to himself"* (v. 27).

If a man is to do this for his wife, he needs to be filled with the Word, just as Christ is filled with the Word. He needs to wash his wife with the Word, just as Christ washes His bride with the Word. Now, you can't wash if you don't have any water. Jesus emphasized the importance of the Word in our lives. He said to His disciples in John 15:3, *"You are already clean because of the word I have spoken to you."* He said to the woman at the well, *"If you knew the gift of God and who it is that asks you for a drink, you would have asked him and he would have given you living water"* (John 4:10).

A MAN NEEDS TO WASH HIS WIFE WITH THE WORD.

A male who wants to be a real man—the man God created him to be—has to be full of the Word of God. There's only one way to get clean water: go to the Well. You can't wash with the muddy water of the world. When you fill your mind and heart only with things such as television or sporting events, that's mud. If you want water that the Manufacturer intended you to have, you need to stay connected to the well of God, which is filled with the Word. Jesus is the Word.

Some men are washing their wives in mud. What does it mean to wash somebody with the Word? Jesus is our Example: every time you have a negative experience, He comes in immediately with a positive one and washes it off. Whenever the disciples were afraid, He said, *"Be of good cheer."* (See, for example, Matthew 14:27 KJV.) Every time they became nervous, He told them to remain calm. Whenever they became frightened by a storm, He told them to relax. He was always there to wash away fear, to wash away doubt. When they wondered how they were going to feed the five thousand, He told them to have faith. When they told Him that Lazarus had died, He said, "Don't worry about it; he's sleeping." He was always washing His church.

What kind of man do we need today? When your wife says, "We can't pay our phone bill," you say, "Our God is bigger than any phone company." That's washing your wife. When your wife says, "We're not going to be able to meet the note at the bank. They're going to repossess the car, and the children are going to be taken out of private school," you say, "Honey, we serve the God of Abraham, Isaac, and Jacob, the God of my grandparents and parents. Let's just keep standing on the Word. It's going to be all right." When your wife feels a little pain in her body and begins to imagine all kinds of things, such as cancer, you have to be there and say, "Honey, God is the God who heals you. Come here and let me pray for you."

Some men have only bad news. "Honey, pack up. We have to move to lesser quarters." They have nothing positive to say—no Scripture, no faith. God wants men who will stand up in their faith, saying, "A thousand may fall on my right, and ten thousand on my left, but in this house we're going to come through with flying colors. My house is covered by the Word of God. As for me and my house, we're going to be all right." That's a man. That's a washer. However, he can do that only if he is filled with the Word.

A Partner in God's Creation

The male has been given the serious but exciting responsibility of shaping the lives of his family members for the better—teaching and cultivating them to be all that God created them to be. In this way, he is a partner with God in fulfilling His plan of creation. Two more assignments in which a man reflects his Creator are that of provider and protector. We'll explore these responsibilities in the next chapter.

PRINCIPLES

1. The male was created to be the spiritual leader and teacher of his family.

2. The male has been designed with the capacity to fulfill his purpose of teaching.

3. When you teach your family God's Word and ways, you attract God's trust and friendship.

4. If a man doesn't have the knowledge and capacity to teach a woman the Word, he's not ready for marriage.

5. God instructs men to teach their families His commandments in these ways: (1) when you sit at home, (2) when you walk along the road, (3) when you lie down, (4) when you get up, and (5) by tying them as symbols on your hands, binding them on your foreheads, and writing them on the doorframes of your houses and gates. (See Deuteronomy 6:7–9.)

6. The male was created to be the cultivator of the spiritual and personal lives of his family members.

7. To cultivate means to multiply, make fruitful, make better.

8. The male is the cultivator of his work, talents, and skills.

9. The male is the cultivator of his children.

10. The male is the cultivator of his wife.

11. A man needs to be filled with the Word, just as Christ is filled with the Word. Then he can wash his wife with the Word, just as Christ washes His bride with His Word.

12. The male has been given the responsibility of shaping the lives of his family members for the better—teaching and cultivating them to be all that God created them to be. In this way, the male is a partner with God in fulfilling His plan of creation.

8

THE MALE AS PROVIDER AND PROTECTOR

GOD HAS GIVEN MEN THE ABILITY TO PROVIDE FOR AND
PROTECT EVERYTHING HE HAS ENTRUSTED TO THEIR CARE.

T he two dominion assignments of provider and protector are interrelated because they work together to enable a man to secure himself and those who are under his care.

THE MALE AS PROVIDER

In Genesis 2:15, God gave the male the assignment of work: *"The LORD God took the man and put him in the Garden of Eden to work it and take care of it."* As we saw earlier, work was given prior to the fall of man. It is not a curse; on the contrary, it is a great blessing. Genesis 1:28 says that God blessed the male and female and gave them dominion over the earth. He blessed them in all their dominion assignments—including work.

Work was given to the male (1) to advance the purposes of God, (2) to bring the male fulfillment while using the skills and abilities God has given him, and (3) to enable the male to provide for his own needs as well as the needs of those for whom he is responsible. In an earlier chapter, we learned that a male's first priority is to remain continually in God's presence. It is through worship and communion with God that the man receives his life's vision, vocation, and work. Some men have forgotten that worship takes precedence over work. When your work interferes with your worship, you cease to fulfill the purpose of a real man.

CREATED TO PROVIDE

Man was given work before the woman was created. This means that before a man needs a woman, and before he is ready for marriage, he needs work. He needs to find out what God is calling him to do. Then he can use his vocation and work to provide for his future wife and children.

Note that God never told the woman to work. Now, don't get nervous. You say, "But society has progressed. Women want to work in jobs outside the home. There is equality." Sometimes you can have "progress" without real advancement. What are some of the symptoms of both men and women working outside the home? We're experiencing them right now. We have bigger houses, but fewer real homes. Husbands and wives are so busy that they end up like ships passing in the night. We have more furniture, but no one is sitting in it because people have no time to come together as families. Our children's beds are empty because they're out doing drugs. Parents aren't taking the time to mentor them. We have nicer cars, but they are being used to take family members to separate destinations instead of bringing them together. You can say anything you want, but we have to carefully reconsider the expectation that women should work. We have to turn things around in our society.

BEFORE A MAN NEEDS A WOMAN, HE NEEDS WORK.

God gave the man, not the woman, the responsibility for being the main provider of the family. A woman is supposed to marry someone who is already able to provide. This is very important. If you look at the Old Testament Scriptures, the way in which God's people married indicates what God instructed them to do regarding matrimony.

If a man was interested in a woman, he didn't go to her to get engaged. He went to her parents—more specifically, to her father. The resulting marriage contract included specific arrangements for the woman's provision. The father would establish the standard of living that the man would have to provide for his daughter before he would allow her to leave his household. The prospective groom would have to show that he could meet this standard, or he would have to earn the money before he could have her hand in marriage.

Sometimes this took years. Remember the story of Jacob? He was engaged for seven years, but he ended up working fourteen years for Rachel. How many of you could make it through an engagement of that length? Let me tell you how easy it is to be engaged for seven years. Just have a contract like that. You'd be so busy earning that money, you wouldn't have time to get into any trouble. A woman also wouldn't have to worry about her husband leaving her. If he'd spend seven years *without* her, working for her, he'd be more likely to spend seventy years *with* her, working for her.

There is much we can learn from this system. We might not want to return to everything about it, but the point is that males must fully understand the importance of their being responsible for providing for their wives and families.

Some women are locked into providing because they didn't meet a provider; they met a schemer. Certain men are with women because the women have good jobs—and the men want to be supported by them. They don't want to be the providers they were created to be.

Many women who are working today don't really want to work full time outside the home. Women going to college and having careers has been a positive change in many ways. Women need to be able to develop their talents and abilities. However, they should be able to do so with joy, not stress. Many women are juggling so many things today—career, home, family—that working a job can be a tremendous strain on them and the rest of the family. Some women are stuck in dead-end jobs rather than fulfilling ones because they feel the family needs the money they provide. They're not working at what they would really like to do. In addition, when women start having children, work doesn't usually retain the same priority with them. When their first baby comes, they want to be at home to care for him or her. They forget their work and the people at the office. Many women are now saying openly

MANY WOMEN TODAY DON'T WANT TO WORK FULL TIME OUTSIDE THE HOME.

that they want to be homemakers. They want to have time to care for their husbands and children.

I know there are certain men reading this section who are becoming uncomfortable and discouraged. They're not lazy—they're just going through hard economic times. I understand how you feel. You don't want your wife to work, but right now you need two incomes to make ends meet. Or right now you're trying to find a job. Don't be discouraged. We won't always be able to change our financial circumstances overnight.

WE CAN'T ALWAYS CHANGE OUR FINANCIAL SITUATIONS OVERNIGHT— WE JUST NEED TO MOVE TOWARD THE IDEAL.

We just need to move toward the ideal by beginning to turn things around. You can tell your wife, "Sweetheart, you're working now, but my goal is to make enough money so you don't have to work. I will start working on it right now."

DESIGNED TO PROVIDE

Now, since a male was created to work, he was also designed to work. He has an inherent need for it. Many women wonder how a man can work all day and all night and then some. A wife may say, "Leave that job and come home," and her husband will answer, "Just let me finish this." She's thinking about the food on the table that's getting cold. "Come home now." "Yes, baby, but let me finish this one thing." What does this tendency say about him? It says that he derives satisfaction from completing his work—from "conquering" a task. Many men will tell you they feel that way about their jobs.

A PROVIDER PLANS AND PREPARES

A provider finds a way to supply the needs of his family. He makes preparations to fulfill his responsibilities. This means that in order to find a good job, a man may need to explore career options, go back to school, or get additional training.

A provider also plans ahead. The problem with many men today is that they operate in crisis mode. They wait for financial problems to come to them instead of sitting down and planning for the needs of their families five or ten years in advance. A provider anticipates needs before they arrive. A loving husband is always thinking about what his wife is going to need tomorrow, and he plans for it today.

This is the kind of Husband that Jesus is for His bride, the church. Before you or I were created, He prepared for our salvation. He is *"the Lamb that was slain from the creation of the world"* (Rev. 13:8). Jesus made arrangements for our need because He cares deeply for us. He anticipated and met our need before it arose. That is what caring is all about.

If a man's planning nature isn't guided by the Spirit of Christ, it can become destructive rather than constructive. That's when you see men planning crimes and taking advantage of women. They plan these things out—sometimes for a long time. They usually don't just happen.

THE NEEDS OF A PROVIDER

Built into the male's desire to work and provide is his need to give. We learned earlier that the male was designed essentially as a giver and the female essentially as a receiver. The male needs someone to receive what he has to give. If he has no one to give to, this affects how he feels about himself as a man. Many women today think of themselves as independent, but they need to learn to receive from their husbands, fiancés, or boyfriends. They need to learn what it means to men to be able to give to them—and they should allow them to do it. Being a provider can sometimes be just a role for some men, but giving is a function related to a male's design and need.

BUILT INTO THE MALE'S DESIRE TO WORK AND PROVIDE IS HIS NEED TO GIVE.

God designed the male to gain satisfaction from both working and providing. When he's able to do these two things, he's a happy man. If you want to undermine a man's nature, then provide for him instead of letting him provide. That may sound strange, because some men just want to loaf. But most men aren't like that. If a wife tells a husband he doesn't need to buy her groceries, that she doesn't need him to do anything for her anymore, she's dealing a blow to an essential part of his being.

If you are a women who is educated and has a good job, you need to be careful. You may be tempted to say—or at least to imply—to your husband, "I don't need you or anything you have. You're lucky I married you." You don't know how this affects him. The man is designed to be a provider; therefore, no matter how much money you earn, make sure you keep encouraging him as a provider. Do it in a way that he doesn't even know you're doing it. Then let him bless you with what he gives you. Whenever a man feels like he isn't providing, you will probably have an unhappy household.

Many women don't understand the mental, emotional, and spiritual effect that losing a job has on a man. They cannot fully understand, because they are not designed to be providers; they are designed to be producers. When a man loses his job, it's as if his life has fallen apart. Some men actually end up losing their minds after they lose their jobs. Why do they have such an extreme reaction? It's because it's not just a job to them. It's their means of providing. One of their purposes for being has been taken away from them.

WHEN A MAN LOSES HIS JOB, IT'S AS IF HIS LIFE HAS FALLEN APART.

When a man thinks, "I can't provide," he sometimes skips town. Some men can't handle that kind of pressure, so they run from responsibility. Maybe the man has six kids and can't feed them. He feels useless; he feels like a failure, so he leaves. We call his behavior neglectful or irresponsible. Although this behavior is wrong, we must realize that the man is dealing with something internal that he may not understand, something fundamental to his being.

Suppose a man calls his wife and says, "Sweetheart, I have some bad news for you. I just got laid off from my job." This is how some women would react: "I'm not surprised. You haven't been able to hold a job for the last six months.

As a matter of fact, ever since I married you, I've been carrying the family." What has she done by saying this? She has just made his bed somewhere else. He feels humiliated and unwanted. He doesn't want to go home to that. Instead, she should say something like, "Well, honey, God says that He's our Source. I've always believed that if God made you my covering, He'll provide for you so you can provide for us. As a matter of fact, I love you for who you are, not because of the things you buy me. Hello? Are you there?"

A MAN NEEDS HIS WIFE TO RESPECT HIS DESIRE TO PROVIDE.

"Yes, honey, you just make me so proud to have you as my wife. You make me feel so much like a man. I'll be home in five seconds." When he arrives, she can greet him at the door and say, "Sweetheart, job or no job, you're the best thing that ever happened to me." You want to see a man go get a job the next morning? Whatever he can get, even if it's sweeping the streets, he'll do it. What did his wife do for him? She restored his confidence. She gave him respect and elevated him as the head of the home all in one sentence. And now she has a provider who will continue to provide.

THE MALE AS PROTECTOR

When God told Adam to take care of the Garden (Gen. 2:15), He was telling him, in effect, "I put you in the Garden not only to work and cultivate it, but also to protect it and everything in it—including the animals, the plants, and the woman I will create. You are a protector."

CREATED TO PROTECT

The male is like God's "security guard." When he shows up, everyone is supposed to feel protected and safe. Remember that the atmosphere of God's Garden is His presence. Therefore, God essentially told Adam, "Protect the Garden, but also the presence that is in it. Don't let anything disturb My presence here." It is up to males to maintain God's presence—whether they are at their homes, jobs, or any other place in society. They are to be protectors.

I can hear some men saying, "I can't wait until I get married so I can practice what he's teaching." Don't wait until then. In 1 Corinthians 11:3, Paul said, *"The head of the woman is man."* This means that a man doesn't need to be married to be responsible for women. Start being the protector of every female who comes into your presence, because you were created to be responsible for her.

Any women should feel safe with you when you understand that your purpose is to protect and guard her and to lead her into the things of God. What should happen if a woman comes to you destitute, broken, depressed, sad, and vulnerable, and she confides in you? The spirit of protection should come upon you. Lead her straight to God. Show her Jesus. Then exemplify His character by treating her in a fatherly or brotherly way.

A MAN DOESN'T NEED TO BE MARRIED TO BE RESPONSIBLE FOR WOMEN.

Men, when you are dating, you don't protect a woman by throwing away your own armor. You don't take her for a drive at night and park in a secluded place. Keep the lights on bright. Keep the tape playing the Word of God. Keep the conversation in the light.

It takes a real man to keep his hands to himself. That's true strength. A man once said to me, "Brother Myles, it's so tough living right." "Why?" "All those girls, mmm-mmm. They have those short skirts and high boots and bikinis. It's hard working in a hotel. You don't understand." It takes a stronger man to say no to all that than to fall for it. Any weak man can allow his hormones to run his life.

Now, when a woman gets married, her husband becomes her protector, as her father was. Because of her nature, she needs the covering of protection. The male is to provide everything for her: security, covering, resources, counsel, the comfort of knowing that he's there for her.

A man's wife and children are supposed to feel totally at peace in his presence. As soon as he shows up, everything is in order. When they hear his voice, everything is all right. When a daughter gets hurt, her father's presence makes her feel better. When a son goes away to college, becomes homesick, and feels as if his life is falling apart, he can call his father and hear him say, "Son, it's going to be okay." Suddenly everything comes into place because Dad spoke a reassuring word. When a wife becomes frustrated or emotional about what's happening in the family, her husband can say, "God says He'll be here for us, and I will be here for us, too." That's a man's responsibility.

DESIGNED TO PROTECT

A male is a natural protector. Through these attributes, he is designed to protect everything he is responsible for:

1. physical strength
2. logical thinking
3. a sense of territorial protectiveness
4. a drive to excel or "ego"

1. PHYSICAL STRENGTH

The male's bone structure and upper body strength is designed to defend, protect, and guard. Now, even if a man isn't tall or extremely muscular, he seems to have inner physical resources that enable him to defend. A man's wife should be able to run to him any time trouble comes. "Only 102 pounds, but that's my man. If you touch me, he'll have your head."

The safest place for a woman should be in the arms of her husband. Yet one of the saddest things I've seen is men abusing their strength. Instead of using it to protect women, they use it to destroy them. When I think of a man hitting a woman, my whole body turns into a boiling pot of indignation. God gave him muscles to protect her, not to hurt her.

Paul said that a man should love his wife as Christ Jesus loves His church: as his own flesh. Can you imagine Jesus slapping His church? I have a little recommendation to all men who are tempted to physically abuse women: any time you feel like slapping or hitting them, do the exact thing to yourself first. After a couple of hits, you won't hit anybody. Any man who beats a woman is abusing his God-given faculties.

The other day I counseled a forty-year-old man who was sexually abusing his thirteen-year-old daughter. Here's this man, with all his strength, abusing a girl who is his own flesh. She can't cry out or fight because he's too strong for her. He's supposed to use his strength to protect her from the very thing he's doing. Sometimes males wonder why so many women have problems with men. It is because a man's strength is frightening to them. They grew up seeing this strength being used *against* them or their mothers— instead of *for* them, as it was intended to be used.

GOD GAVE MEN STRENGTH TO PROTECT— NOT ABUSE.

2. A LOGICAL THINKER

Second, God created the male as a logical thinker. This enables him to face difficulties and danger with a clear mind and without emotional distractions, so that he can find solutions to these problems. How does he exercise this logical thinking?

A male scrutinizes. He checks out people and things before making a decision about them. For example, men usually don't join a church right away. They will sit in the back and observe. They will examine things to see if what's going on is real. They will wait to see if the pastor is genuine. Women accept things more quickly, but men scrutinize.

A male also analyzes. To analyze means not only to see something, but also to try to interpret what it means. A woman will see a healing and say, "That's a miracle," but a man will say, "Miracle? I don't think she was sick at all. She was just sick in her mind." He analyzes things. That's just the way men are.

Third, a male is very precise in his planning. A man will look at something and plan how he will approach it. Women can be spontaneous, but men will consider things and say, "If I go in there, I have to make sure this is okay."

Fourth, a male thinks of consequences. "When I do this, I can do that," or "If they do that, I can do this." He looks at opportunities, results, and outcomes of actions.

When a man loses his job and can't pay the mortgage or other bills, he shouldn't fall apart and go drinking, use drugs, or run away. God intended a real man to be able to look at life's challenges squarely in the face and make a plan of action. "Well, let's see what size this one is. Good. I can knock this one off. It will take three weeks, but I'll do it." "This other one isn't too bad. In three months we'll work on that one." "Well, now, for this one, we'll have to go to the bank and make some arrangements for smaller payments so we'll have more time to deal with it."

The logical thinker was built to handle tough things. A man looks trouble in the face and says, "No problem." He speaks with confidence because he's logical, and his logic is based on God's Word.

3. TERRITORIAL PROTECTIVENESS

Males exhibit a fighting spirit, which was given to them by God to protect and defend those for whom they are responsible. Jesus said, *"O Jerusalem, Jerusalem,...how often I have longed to gather your children together, as a hen gathers her chicks under her wings"* (Matt. 23:37). When does a hen cover her chicks? When there's a threat. She opens her wing, covers them with it, then starts kick-

JESUS EXHIBITED A STRONG, PROTECTIVE NATURE.

ing with her foot. She is saying, "Don't you touch my chicks." That's how God feels about His people. Likewise, a man has the spirit of a hen who is under pressure and threat of danger, and who is going to fight.

Jesus exhibited a strong, protective nature when speaking of the church. He said, in essence, "If anyone offends My bride, if anyone tries to take My children away from Me, it would be better for him if he tied a rope around his neck, put a stone on the other end of the rope, walked down to the ocean, and jumped in. It would be better for him to do that than for Me to get My hands on him." (See Matthew 18:6.)

A man has a spirit in him that says, "I have to protect what is mine." He talks in terms of "my wife," "my house," and "my car." This possessive attitude isn't negative in itself; it's from God. However, when it is not submitted to its pur-

MEN ARE MEANT TO FIGHT AGAINST SIN AND SATAN, NOT FLESH AND BLOOD.

pose, it is often used to overpower or control others. For example, a man might end up ruling his wife as if she's his property. A man like this doesn't want anybody to even come near his wife. If he just imagines that she might be unfaithful, he goes into a rage. Why? He doesn't want anybody interfering with his territory. Some men will actually kill their wives for infidelity, even though they themselves have been unfaithful for years. They don't understand their purpose, so they abuse it.

Some young men don't know what to do with their spirit of possessiveness and competition, so they end up forming gangs and competing against other neighborhoods. They are aggressive against others who don't wear the same hat or jacket they do. They need strong male role models who can teach them what to do with their territorial protectiveness.

Jesus got angry many times, but His anger was aimed at ungodliness and hypocrisy. The Bible says, *"For this purpose the Son of God was manifested, that he might destroy the works of the devil"* (1 John 3:8 KJV). Men aren't supposed to fight against other men, but against the spiritual forces that try to steal what God told them to protect. They are to compete against the sinful nature and satan, not flesh and blood. A real man has righteous indignation. He is protective of that which is holy. He safeguards what is good.

Nothing in the world can bless a man like feeling responsible for his family's safety. For instance, something happens within him when he can provide his wife and children with a house. He has kept them safe from the elements. He's built a place for them, and he feels proud. "My house is only two rooms, you know, but it's my house." When a man provides his wife with a car, and the car breaks down, he feels instantly protective. He can't stand to think of her out there in the elements, and he immediately goes and takes care of the situation.

160

You wouldn't imagine how much it hurts a man to feel as if he has no part in protecting his wife and children, to feel as if he's just visiting in his own home—eating and sleeping there but not contributing to his family's welfare. It is important for men to participate in solving family problems. When something happens in the home or to the children, a wife should tell her husband. Why? He needs to fulfill his dominion purpose as protector.

His wife needs to encourage him in this purpose. Suppose a man opens a door for his wife but she says, "That's okay, I'm liberated." She has just insulted his protective nature. Now, because of the way male-female relationships are changing in our societies, men don't know whether they should open a door for a woman or not. They're confused, so many have stopped doing it altogether. Sometimes we men need to be reminded of our assignment. I'll tell the women what they should do in this situation. My wife is an expert at this. She goes outside and stands beside the car. I get in the car and she's still standing there. Then it hits me. "Oh, right." I get out, go back around, and open the door for her.

SOME MEN CHECK ON THEIR INVESTMENTS MORE THAN THEY DO THEIR FAMILIES.

Some men have lost sight of their responsibility to protect to such an extent that they check on their investments more often than they check to see if their families are all right. These men are using their natural gift of protectiveness, but they're using it on the wrong objects. A man should call his wife every day, making sure everything is okay. "Is anybody bothering you?" He should also call to see how his children are doing, so they can know their father is there for them. A man's spirit of territorial protection is to be used primarily to safeguard his family and others under his care.

4. A Drive to Excel or "Ego"

Finally, God gave the male what psychologists call *ego*. I like to call it a drive to excel. The man's ego is simply a spirited attitude of not wanting to be beaten. God gave him this attitude to help him overcome obstacles in life. Nothing makes a woman prouder than to see her mighty man of valor standing against the odds. Every male is supposed to have this spirit. When he doesn't, he's not fully functioning.

A male always wants to outdo. This is one reason men are so competitive. Sports are more attractive to males than females because they provide a release for this drive to excel. For example, many men have a basketball team that they call their own. Maybe it's the Lakers or the Bullets. These men don't play on those teams, practice with them, or even watch them work out, but they relish the competition they represent. A man may never have visited Los Angeles, but when the Lakers win, he'll have a celebration. He never played basketball in his life, but he's as proud of their accomplishments as if he were part of the team himself.

A MAN'S EGO NEEDS TO BE BUILT ON THE WORD.

A man isn't meant to release his drive to excel just on the basketball court. There are men who can shoot a three-pointer, but who don't bring up their children to rely on the Lord. There are men who have all kinds of sports trophies, but who haven't learned to take their drive and channel it properly through the Word of God, using faith to feed it. The mark of a man who knows God is, "I know I can make it, and nobody can stop me."

So ego, in itself, is not a bad thing. Having a drive to excel is good because it's part of a man's equipment for leadership. When a man has to bring his family through a difficult situation, he'd better have some ego. He'd better believe in himself to the point that he can say, "This thing can't overcome me. My God will supply all my needs." He can be confident because He trusts in God's provision. He can be strong because He believes he is everything that God says he is in Christ. That's the definition of a redeemed ego.

Ego needs to be built on the Word, but when it has been corrupted by sin, satan uses it to tempt men to connive, scheme, and even kill one other. That's not what God intended. God gave men a drive to excel so they be good examples for their children of how to be faithful during tough times. God gave men ego so they can constantly come forth with more motivation and more hope for life's battles—to be able to keep moving when everything and everyone else quits. A wife whose husband has this drive to excel can say, "It doesn't matter what happens out there. He's not going to fold up." So you lose your job. Your ego should be so big that you walk back home and say, "I got laid off today, but that must mean God has something better for me."

Men, no matter how difficult your life becomes, I want you to know you have what it takes to handle it. God designed you to come through storms and to work out problems. He has given you everything you need to be a man of God. He has given you His own Spirit. In the Bible, the men who trusted God were full of hope. They always knew they were going to come through. God has given you wonderful ability, strength, and spiritual weaponry to protect and guard everything He has entrusted to your care.

COMMIT TO BECOMING GOD'S MAN

Men must understand that they are responsible for their purpose assignments. The whole revelation has to hit you: "As a male, I am a visionary, leader, teacher, cultivator, provider, and protector." Being the male that God designed you to be means all these things.

A male doesn't decide to work—he's designed to work. He doesn't decide to teach—he's required to teach. He cannot decide to protect—He is wired to protect. There is no fulfillment without satisfying your purpose. My prayer is that you will commit to becoming the man God created and designed you to be so that you will experience lasting fulfillment in your relationship with God and in all your human relationships. *"See to it that you complete the work you have received in the Lord"* (Col. 4:17). Work on becoming a complete man of God, and you will be a blessing to yourself, your family, and the world.

PRINCIPLES

1. The male was created to be the provider of his family.

2. Work was given to the male (1) to advance the purposes of God, (2) to bring the male fulfillment while using the skills and abilities God has given him, and (3) to enable the male to provide for his own needs as well as the needs of those for whom he is responsible.

3. Man was given work before the woman was created. This means that before a man needs a woman, and before he is ready for marriage, he needs work.

4. God gave the man, not the woman, the responsibility for being the main provider of the family.

5. A husband won't always be able to immediately change his financial circumstances so that his wife doesn't have to work. He just needs to move toward the ideal by working toward this goal.

6. Since a male was created to provide, he was also designed to provide.

7. A provider anticipates needs before they arrive. He plans, prepares, and makes provision for these needs.

8. Built into the male's desire to work and provide is his need to give.

9. The male was created to be the protector of his family and everything else for which he is responsible.

10. In 1 Corinthians 11:3, Paul said, *"The head of the woman is man."* This means a man doesn't need to be married to be responsible for women.

11. Through these attributes, a male is designed to protect everything he is responsible for: (1) physical strength, (2) logical thinking, (3) a sense of territorial protectiveness, and (4) a drive to excel or "ego."

12. God has given men the ability, strength, and spiritual weaponry to protect and guard everything He has entrusted to their care.

9

A MAN AND HIS SEX LIFE

SEX IS A PHYSICAL SIGN OF A SPIRITUAL ACT—THE GIVING
OF ONESELF COMPLETELY TO ANOTHER
AND FOR ANOTHER.

U nderstanding the sexual nature of the male is essential for any man who wants to know his purpose in God. Unfortunately, sexuality is often extremely misunderstood—not only in the world, but also in the church. I am deeply concerned about the damage this lack of understanding about sex has done—and is doing—to people's lives. It has led to confusion, misunderstanding, and broken relationships between men and women. It has prevented males from living up to their full potential as men and husbands. It has destroyed marriages—and lives. My prayer is that men and women will find wholeness in God as they understand His purpose and plan for human sexuality.

HOW WE LEARN ABOUT SEX

How did you first learn about sexuality? When I've asked men in my seminars how they were introduced to the concept of sex, they've listed various sources, such as:

- friends or peers
- movies and television
- books about biology
- pornographic magazines or videos
- sexual experimentation during youth

Unfortunately, most of us were introduced to sex through one of these avenues. No one ever says he learned about sex from his parents. Something is very wrong with how we are learning about sexuality. Look at the above list again. Note that not one of these sources is qualified to provide accurate information:

Friends or peers: Friends provide mainly hearsay. They are still trying to figure out what sex is all about themselves.

Movies and television: Many people experience sexual frustration because they have developed wrong ideas and unrealistic expectations from watching movies and television. The nature of the entertainment media is fantasy, and its depiction of sexuality is often false and destructive to real relationships.

Books on biology: These books provide mainly the technical aspects of the experience. They don't describe the emotional, psychological, and spiritual aspects.

Pornographic magazines or videos: Pornography is designed to promote sexual fantasy and deviation—to addict people to it, in order to perpetuate the porn industry. Its purpose is to make money rather than to instruct. As a matter of fact, if you were to follow its suggestions, you would subject yourself and whomever you're involved with to perversion. Pornographic images are especially dangerous because they often become imprinted on people's minds and can be a spiritual stronghold.

Experimentation during youth: Experimenting with sex with no understanding of its purpose and nature is no way for a young person to be introduced to something as precious and as dangerous as sex. Moreover, when you participate in something, you are creating a capacity for it. When you create a capacity for it, you want to satisfy that desire. Yet once the desires have been created, your appetite for them grows. It increases by use.

IGNORANCE ABOUT SEXUALITY

How a person has learned about sex determines, to a large extent, how he engages in it. Some of you are suffering right now from the consequences of uninformed or unwise sexual activity.

When we receive our information about sex from one or more of the above sources, then pass along this information to others, we perpetuate cultural ignorance about sexuality. This is what has been happening in our societies. Much of what we have learned about sex has been acquired in an unwholesome context, and it is filled with misinformation. Men and women lack positive, informed teaching on the subject of sexuality.

Much of the blame for this lack of teaching rests with the church and the home. In general, the message we've heard from our churches and families is that sex is unholy or dirty and should not be discussed. Have you ever gone to church and heard the minister say, "Our message today is sex"? If that were to happen, people might be shocked, but I don't believe they would leave. People are really hurting in the area of sexuality, and they want to know what God has to say about it. Yet somehow

THE MESSAGE WE'VE LEARNED FROM CHURCH AND HOME IS THAT SEX IS UNHOLY AND SHOULDN'T BE DISCUSSED.

the church has decided it's not proper to discuss the topic. In addition, young people get the idea that parents and children aren't supposed to talk about sex, because their own parents didn't discuss it with them. In this way, they are prevented from expressing their sexual questions in the context of a loving home or church community, and they seek information from other sources.

What can we do? First, we shouldn't condemn ourselves for the situation we're in, because this is the way we were brought up, and this is also how most of our parents were raised. The answer lies in renewing our minds by God's Word—for the sake of our own sexual wholeness, and so our children will not grow up receiving sexual instruction from unqualified and harmful sources, but rather from parents who understand God's plan for sexuality.

No one has a right to shape your child's concept and attitudes about sex, except you. Make sure that a questionable sex education class or *Playboy* isn't your child's teacher. Train your child in the way he should go. Then, when a friend or teacher starts to say something erroneous about sex, your child can dismiss it, with the knowledge, "That isn't what my parents told me."

GOD CREATED SEX

First, we must realize that God is not negative about sex. He *created* it. (See Genesis 1:28.) Sex is God's idea, not man's idea. It is such a beautiful expression of love and giving that only God could have thought of it. Men and women were designed as sexual beings. Every baby is born as a sexual creature with the potential to have a sexual relationship as an adult. God is negative only about the *misuse* of sex, because it harms the people He created to have a fulfilling relationship with the opposite sex. Second, we must realize that the Bible itself is very open about the subject of sexuality. The main theme of the book of Song of Solomon is sexual love.

Why did God create sex? The primary reason is that unity is a central aspect of God's nature and purposes. In the Bible, the sexual union of marriage is used as a metaphor to describe the intimacy between Christ and the church. Christ being called the Bridegroom and the church being called the bride gives us an idea of the preciousness with which God views sex. It as a symbol of His oneness with His beloved humanity, who have been created in His image and redeemed through His love.

SEX IS GOOD

How do we know that sex is a good thing? Genesis 1:31 says, *"God saw all that he had made, and it was very good."* God created man and woman and their sexual nature. Therefore, He said that sex is *"very good."*

Those who have studied the human body say that the most pleasurable physical experience in life is sexual climax. It can hardly be compared with anything else. Yet today, the misuse of sex has become one of the worst enemies of man. It is the cause of broken homes, illegitimate children, child pornography, and billions of dollars worth of government social programs. What God designed to be a high and good pleasure has become a base element of destruction. We must regain an understanding of God's good purposes for sexuality.

The Sexual Design

God designed sex within marriage for these reasons: (1) to procreate the human race, (2) to seal a blood covenant between two humans, and (3) to allow sex to be enjoyed to its maximum potential without repercussions.

1. To Procreate the Human Race

After God created male and female (Gen. 1:27), He blessed them and said, *"Be fruitful and increase in number; fill the earth and subdue it"* (v. 28). There is only one way to *"be fruitful and increase in number."* God was telling them, in effect, "Go for it. Don't just have a few children. Fill the earth."

2. To Seal a Blood Covenant between Two Humans

The Bible says, *"A man will leave his father and mother and be united to his wife, and they will become one flesh"* (Gen. 2:24). Sexual intercourse constitutes making yourself *"one flesh"* with another person. This term refers to a fleshly (physical) or sexual covenant.

Did you know that the covering of the female's vagina has no biological or medical purpose? Yet medical science has discovered that that little layer of skin has one of the highest concentrations of blood vessels in the body. The only thing that comes from that layer of skin is blood.

Let's think about the significance of this fact. The strongest form of covenant in the Bible is the blood covenant, and God has designed the sexual experience as a type of blood covenant. That is why sex must be engaged in only in the context of marriage—a solemn, lifelong commitment between two people before God. That is also why there are such serious warnings in Scripture concerning not having sex with just anybody. The Scripture says that if you have sex with a prostitute, you have joined yourself to her in a covenant. Even after you've paid her the money and gone, you still remain with her in some sense—and she with you.

THE SEXUAL EXPERIENCE IS A COVENANT.

3. TO ALLOW SEX TO BE ENJOYED TO ITS MAXIMUM POTENTIAL WITHOUT REPERCUSSIONS

In Deuteronomy, we find a remarkable Scripture: *"If a man has recently married, he must not be sent to war or have any other duty laid on him. For one year he is to be free to stay at home and bring happiness to the wife he has married"* (Deut. 24:5). That is God's Word.

Imagine, God wanted young married couples to enjoy sex so much that He issued a decree to ensure that it was provided for. The very thing we think God is against, He promoted. A newly married man was to have no other responsibilities during his first year of marriage but to bring his wife happiness. He would stay with her and just bless her. I think we should adopt that provision today.

GOD CREATED SEX FOR PLEASURE—NOT REPERCUSSIONS AND REMORSE.

Note that it doesn't say the husband is to bring happiness to himself, but to his wife. Lust focuses on itself, but true love focuses on the other person. God was saying to the husband, "Your desire in marriage should be to make your wife happy." Now, when you make your wife happy, guess who wins? You both do. When you give, you receive.

God established marriage so the sexual relationship can be full of pleasure—not repercussions and remorse. God is not against sex. He's against the violation of the sexual boundaries He's established for our own good.

In order to fulfill our highest potential, we have to follow the laws that God gave us. Men, if you can grasp this point, you'll understand how easy it is to live in a godly way in the area of sexuality. God's laws are for our protection, not our restriction. His boundaries have been established for our preservation, not our irritation. We think God doesn't want us to have any fun. In reality, He is really trying to protect us. Whenever we break a law or violate a principle of God, we invite spiritual death and suffering.

PROTECTIVE BOUNDARIES OF SEXUALITY

God wants us to enjoy sex so much that He has told us what its safe boundaries are. The primary boundary is the marriage covenant.

The Scripture we just looked at said that a man is to *"bring happiness to the wife he has married"* (Deut. 24:5). It doesn't say to move in with somebody for a year and try things out. There are no provisionary covenants. Solomon said, *"May you rejoice in the wife of your youth....May her breasts satisfy you always, may you ever be captivated by her love"* (Prov. 5:18–19). This passage is a reference to sex. Enjoy *"the wife of your youth"*—not someone else. There is a vacuum in the male that needs to be filled by the female. And God says, "Make sure your wife fills that vacuum."

> [Adam] *said, "This is now bone of my bones and flesh of my flesh; she shall be called 'woman,' for she was taken out of man." For this reason a man will leave his father and mother and be united to his wife, and they will become one flesh.* (Gen. 2:23–24)

"For this reason." For what reason should a man leave? To *"be united."* To whom? His wife. The minute that law is violated, we begin to reap the repercussions. Verse 24 says, *"And they will become one flesh."* The boundaries that God has established for the one-flesh experience is the husband and wife relationship.

Marriage enables us to enjoy sex to the fullest. How does a young man who has just been married feel after he has had sex with his wife on their honeymoon? Totally at peace. He doesn't care if people talk about what he and his wife did. He has no embarrassment about it or fear of being caught. There is so much freedom within the laws of God. Yet when you violate God's laws, the first thing you lose is your peace.

DOING WHAT IS PERMISSIBLE VERSUS BENEFICIAL

In 1 Corinthians 6:12, Paul said, *"Everything is permissible for me."* That means I can do anything I want. Yet he continued, *"But not everything is beneficial."* Your right to do something is not what is important. What's good for you is what's important. Your understanding of the benefits or drawbacks of something allows you to determine if it is good for you.

"The body is not meant for sexual immorality" (v. 13). The Scripture doesn't say the body is not meant for sex. Nor does it say people don't use the body for immorality. It simply says the body is not *meant* for immorality. This is one of God's sexual laws, which He gives us for our good.

Someone may say, "Oh, come on. When a man goes to bed with a woman, whether it's moral or immoral, it feels good." Our justification and rationalization for immorality is, "It feels good." But God says, "I'm not dealing with feeling good. I'm dealing with what your body was made for. It was made for sex, but not for immoral sex."

Something negative happens in a man's body when he has an immoral sexual experience. If the body was not created for it, then something goes wrong when it is subjected to it. This is why a man may feel guilty after such a sexual experience, whether he admits it or not. Men who participate in immorality may even begin to hate their sexual partners, not wanting anything to do with them any longer.

SOMETHING NEGATIVE HAPPENS TO A MAN WHEN HE IS SEXUALLY IMMORAL.

What has happened? Their bodies were not made for immorality. Somehow the knowledge that they broke the law of God is translated into chemicals in their bodies, and they feel bad. Science has proven that there are a few things our bodies are not built to handle. One of them is guilt. Our bodies have no hormone, enzyme, or chemical to handle guilt. Only the blood of Jesus can free us from guilt.

"The body is not meant for sexual immorality, but for the Lord" (v. 13). What is your body made for? It is made for God. It was created to be used in the context that God has already established. God placed specific boundaries on sexual behavior, and we can have all the fun we want within that context. We won't experience these negative repercussions if we stay within God's plan.

Let me say here that God has created males and females to express sexuality in a specific way. God never gave Adam a man; He gave him a woman. God's design is male and female; not male and male, or female and female. We can know that homosexuality is not God's plan because it does not fit His design.

Verse 13 continues, "*And the Lord* [is meant] *for the body.*" The Lord made the body for Himself. God is not against your having sex. In fact, He ought to be present in your marriage to bless your sexual union. Proverbs 10:22 says, "*The blessing of the LORD, it maketh rich, and he addeth no sorrow with it*" (KJV). You can have a rich sex life without sorrow when you follow His plan.

In 1 Corinthians 6:15–18, Paul also said,

> Do you not know that your bodies are members of Christ himself? Shall I then take the members of Christ and unite them with a prostitute? Never! Do you not know that he who unites himself with a prostitute is one with her in body? For it is said, "The two will become one flesh." But he who unites himself with the Lord is one with him in spirit. Flee from sexual immorality.

In the Greek, the word translated *"flee"* means, "Run away. Shun. Escape." In other words, *avoid it like the plague.* How do you respond to plagues? You get as far away from them as you can. You insulate yourself from them.

"*All other sins a man commits are outside his body, but he who sins sexually sins against his own body*" (v. 18). Paul was saying, "If you steal, it is outside the body. If you fight, it is outside the body. If you curse, it is outside the body." You don't become one with a person when you slap or curse that person. But when you have sex with a woman, you can't separate yourself from her. Remember that sexual intercourse is a covenant. Some men can't understand how a couple can sleep together for a time, and then, when they both decide to break off the relationship, they have trouble going their separate ways. It is because the separation causes real trauma in their souls. This is a serious matter. That's why relationships outside God's plan can be so dangerous.

Do you not know that your body is a temple of the Holy Spirit, who is in you, whom you have received from God? You are not your own; you were bought at a price. Therefore honor God with your body. (1 Cor. 6:19–20)

Your body belongs to God twice. He didn't just create you; He also bought you, and the price was high. Your body is God's property. How can you honor God with your body? First, by waiting until you're married to engage in sex, and second, by having sex only with your wife. You are God's temple. You lift up your hands to worship God; you can use those same hands to caress your wife. Both acts are holy in His sight.

WHAT'S LOVE GOT TO DO WITH IT?

Sex is a physical sign of a spiritual act—the giving of oneself completely to another and for another. Marital love is the binding of one spouse to another. Today, people are looking for sex without love, love without marriage, and marriage without responsibility. The world's idea of sex is shallow and distorted. The world says, "Make love." God says, "Love." We have confused sex with love. It's one thing to know how to make love to someone; it's quite another to actually love someone. "Let's make love" refers to a performance. It means to go do something. "Making love" is merely a technical experience, whereas loving is a spiritual act. If sex produced love, no one in the world would feel more love than prostitutes. Yet prostitutes have among the highest rates of suicide.

PEOPLE ARE LOOKING FOR SEX WITHOUT LOVE, LOVE WITHOUT MARRIAGE, AND MARRIAGE WITHOUT RESPONSIBILITY.

Love is the desire to please another, the total giving of oneself to another, not the taking of something. Someone once asked me, "What happens when a person gets married to someone who is an invalid or who is paralyzed? What kind of sex life do they have?" The answer is very simple. They understand that marriage is for love, not just sex. Its foundation should be love. There are many ways to express love and physical affection; sex is just one of them. People can find complete fulfillment in one another without having the technical experience that our culture glorifies so much, because their relationship goes beyond the bedroom. To me, that's a real relationship. *Sex was given by God to help express love, not to create it.*

Anyone who gets married for sexual reasons alone has already paved the way for failure, because sexual desire fluctuates. It grows, peaks, then dies down. If you base your relationship solely on sex, your relationship will also peak and die.

If sex is so important, why does it diminish with age? God expects that as the marriage grows, what we enjoy during the first years of marriage will become less important, and the real relationship will begin to develop. God says, "Enjoy the sexual aspect of your marriage, but move toward an even deeper union as husband and wife based on My unconditional love."

Paul said, *"Husbands, love your wives, just as Christ loved the church and gave himself up for her"* (Eph. 5:25). He was saying, in effect, "The only picture I can use to describe Jesus and the church is the relationship between a devoted husband and wife." The highest witness for Christ that you can give is not preaching, but loving your wife as Christ loved the church.

We need real men in our communities—men of the Word who know what true love is. No one can understand the deep meaning of Jesus and the church better than a man who has a good sexual relationship with his wife. Sexual experience can be a model of Christ's love for His bride, the church, if we follow God's original plan for sexuality.

SEXUAL TRAPS OF MEN

Because sexual sin can be such a temptation for men, I now want to discuss specific sexual traps males fall into and how they can be avoided. Some of you are on the verge of falling into one of these sexual traps. You are going through a crisis you don't want your wife to know about. Yet you can remain faithful to God and your spouse by being aware of these pitfalls and standing strong against them.

Most men want to do what is right. However, many voices beckon them to abandon what is true and good. These voices are the opponents of Christlikeness, self-discipline, and responsibility. They attack men's desire to live righteously. As a man, I am tempted just as you are. We can be kept safe only by knowing what the Word of God says about these temptations and by applying some common sense. Some people think the Holy Spirit is automatically going to keep them from falling into these traps. As we'll see, while the Holy Spirit is always with us to help us, He also expects us to exercise self-control.

TRAP #1: MISUNDERSTANDING THE SEXUAL DIFFERENCE BETWEEN MALES AND FEMALES

We learned in an earlier chapter that the male is physically designed to be a giver. Men are almost *always* ready to give sexually. This is natural. It is how God made them.

The female is physically designed to be a receiver. However, her design is different from the male in that she is not always ready to receive, because her body operates on a cycle. She is more receptive on certain days and at certain times. Because of this tendency, she needs to be treated with kindness and sensitivity by her husband. When men don't understand this sexual difference between males and females, and they expect women to function in the same way they do, they become frustrated. The result can be misunderstanding, resentment, and the desire to look for a person whom they feel will be more receptive.

In addition to her cycle, fatigue and stress may also prevent a woman from being ready to receive. Let's look at things from her viewpoint for a moment. How can a wife be expected to be relaxed, sensitive, and pleasing to her husband right after she comes home from a hard day's work? That is a serious demand. She comes home tired, and her husband expects her to greet him at the door, saying, "Hi, honey. I've been waiting for you. I know you're tired. Take off your shoes, and put your feet up. Here's your big cup of co-coa that you love. Here's the newspaper. The news will be on in thirty minutes. I'm taking the children in the other room so you can listen in peace and quiet. Then I'm going to serve you a five-course dinner because you work so hard all day."

Many men expect this. Yet how can their wives do all that if they are working just as hard as or maybe even harder than their husbands are? It's a tough life. Formerly, when a woman was home all day, she had a little more energy to give to her husband. But nowadays, she needs loving attention herself. Life can be stressful and diffi-cult. You may wonder, "Why is my re-lationship with my wife so tense?" It may be because of the pace and stress of life.

LEARN TO WORK THROUGH YOUR DIFFERENCES WITH PATIENCE AND LOVE.

When a man feels hurt that his wife isn't being as re-ceptive as he would like, he sometimes withdraws from her emotionally, creating a distance between them. This sepa-ration can lead to a sense of rejection by one or both parties that results in many marital problems, including divorce.

To avoid this sexual trap, you need to accept the fact that your wife is different from you, and learn to work through your differences with patience and love. Also, do what you can to alleviate the tension in her life. In this way, she can be more receptive to you, and you will have a more fulfilling relationship. In addition, read 1 Corinthians 13:4–8 and start putting it into practice:

> *Love is patient, love is kind. It does not envy, it does not boast, it is not proud. It is not rude, it is not self-seeking, it is not easily angered, it keeps no record of wrongs. Love does not delight in evil but rejoices with the truth. It always protects, always trusts, always hopes, always perseveres. Love never fails.*

TRAP #2: THE VOICE OF PLEASURE

The voice of pleasure is like the Sirens of Greek mythol-ogy who drew men to their destruction with sweet-sounding songs. Suppose a man has worked in the same job for ten or fifteen years, doing the same routine. After a while, he begins to be attracted to anything he thinks will bring him some pleasure in life.

This is a dangerous situation for a man to be in, because it can lead to infidelity. To avoid this trap, you must be watchful for signs that you are growing weary with life and have started looking to someone other than your wife to bring you pleasure. You must put a guard on your heart and spirit, and look to God for renewal during life's dry spells. Plan to spend extra time with your wife and become reacquainted with her. Talk with your pastor or other trusted Christian men. Go on a spiritual retreat. Ask God for a fresh or renewed vision for your life. Break up your routine with a new interest or goal.

In addition, read and meditate on these verses: *"You have made known to me the path of life; you will fill me with joy in your presence, with eternal pleasures at your right hand"* (Ps. 16:11). *"'For I know the plans I have for you,' declares the LORD, 'plans to prosper you and not to harm you, plans to give you hope and a future'"* (Jer. 29:11).

TRAP #3: THE LURE OF ROMANTICISM

This trap is similar to Trap #2, but it has a subtle difference. It is a search for the romantic or mysterious, in order to bring excitement into a boring lifestyle, put meaning back into life, or dispel a feeling of lost youth. Succumbing to the lure of romanticism makes a man ripe for an extramarital relationship because he thinks that having a romantic relationship with someone new (and therefore "mysterious") will give him an exciting life. The problem is, the new quickly becomes the familiar, and he will soon need something else to create excitement in his life.

You can avoid this sexual trap by following the same advice given in the previous section. In addition, begin to seek God with all your heart. The human desire for excitement and mystery is ultimately meant to be fulfilled in God. There is no one like God, and we will never come to an end of discovering all the facets of His love and character. In addition, read and meditate on these Scriptures: *"God has chosen to make known among the Gentiles the glorious riches of this mystery, which is Christ in you, the hope of glory"* (Col. 1:27). "*[The Lord] redeems your life from the pit and crowns you with love and compassion, [He] satisfies your desires with good things so that your youth is renewed like the eagle's"* (Ps. 103:4–5).

TRAP #4: THE DESIRE FOR EXTRAMARITAL RELATIONSHIPS

Many of you are probably saying to yourselves, "I'm a born-again, Spirit-filled, Bible-toting Christian. I've never thought about an extramarital affair." Let's talk frankly. Men are sexual creatures, and they can be attracted to women other than their wives. A recent study has shown that a man's brain has a physiological response to seeing a beautiful woman that is comparable to his response to food. Apparently, when a man sees a beautiful woman, the "pleasure" circuits in his brain react. This is a physical response, part of a male's design.

Even Christian men who are committed to God and their wives must deal with sexual temptation. Paul admitted that Christians can be tempted in this way when he said in 1 Corinthians 7:5, *"Do not deprive each other except by mutual consent and for a time, so that you may devote yourselves to prayer. Then come together again so that Satan will not tempt you because of your lack of self-control."* Paul was talking to Spirit-filled Corinthian Christians. He was saying, "I know you. You are sexual creatures. Run and find your spouse so you won't be tempted. You're not made of steel."

How can you overcome the trap of desiring an extramarital relationship? First, recognize that your body reacts to physical beauty. Used in the right context, this reaction draws a man to desire the opposite sex and find a life mate. Used in the wrong context, it can lead to infidelity. If you deny this fact, you won't be able to stand strong against temptation.

Second, remember your commitment to God to live a holy life and the covenant you made with your wife. We are not to be ruled by our feelings or hormones, but by the Spirit of God. As a male, I experience the same responses you do.

However, that doesn't mean I'm going to act on them. I have more sense than that. Or, I should say, I have more knowledge than that—knowledge of what God desires for men and women in a marriage covenant.

I have said to my wife, "I see a lot of women who are very nice and attractive, and I could have married them. But I chose you. You're my covenant woman." Marriage is a choice and a commitment. Men are sexual creatures. We see a beautiful woman, and we appreciate beauty, so we say, "Wow, man!" but the Holy Spirit within us says, "Whoa, man!" We need to heed His voice and remain true to our spouses. We shouldn't dwell on tempting thoughts or allow them to control us.

WE SHOULDN'T DWELL ON TEMPTING THOUGHTS OR ALLOW THEM TO CONTROL US.

Third, do not put yourself in a situation where temptation will become too strong for you. As Paul said, stay close to your wife: *"Come together again so that Satan will not tempt you because of your lack of self-control"* (1 Cor. 7:5).

As Christian men, we have to come to grips with this desire for extramarital sexual relations. We need to teach young men that sexual attraction is physiological and shouldn't be acted upon outside the marriage relationship. This knowledge will help to keep them from succumbing to sexual temptation. One of the most honest things men can tell one another is, "Brother, I'm a sexual creature, and I need your support. I need your prayers." We all need each other. Let's help one another stay in God's purposes.

Finally, read and meditate on these verses: *"Guard yourself in your spirit, and do not break faith with the wife of your youth"* (Mal. 2:15). *"Charm is deceptive, and beauty is fleeting; but a woman who fears the LORD is to be praised"* (Prov. 31:30).

TRAP #5: EGO NEED

This last trap is the most dangerous, because the greatest of all influences on men is the ego need. This is the desire to be admired and respected by members of the opposite sex.

I am sure you have experienced this desire before, and you will experience it again. It doesn't matter how much you pray or speak in tongues. If a woman works on your ego needs, you'd better know how to keep yourself pure.

What is harming men in the church right now is a false sense of security based on the idea that once a person is baptized in the Holy Spirit, he is immune from temptations. This just isn't true. The Holy Spirit doesn't give us character; character is something we are responsible for developing. However, He gives us the strength to withstand temptation, to make it through difficulties and to come out on the other side in victory.

Affairs develop because men want to prove they are still attractive to women. The thrill comes from knowing that someone still finds them romantically appealing. It feels good to a man to know that a woman thinks he's intelligent or handsome, that she enjoys talking with him, that she likes the way he thinks, that she finds him exciting to be with. However, if he's a married man, and the woman isn't his wife, he is in a dangerous situation, because his ego need is being stroked.

Attraction based on ego need usually happens gradually, sometimes without either party realizing it's happening. For example, you go to lunch with your secretary and spend just thirty minutes talking with her, but you enjoy her company. Back in the office, she hands you a piece of paper, and you accidentally touch her hand. She smiles. Later, she comes into your office for a report, and says, "You know, I really think you're one of the nicest men I have ever met. If I ever marry a guy, I want him to be just like you." She has made a very innocent statement, and she may be very sincere about it. However, you could now be in trouble, because you are a male, and you have this ego need.

Ego need can make a man behave in foolish and dishonorable ways. It can cause a sane, Spirit-filled, committed, loving Christian man to leave his wife for another woman. He'll say, "This woman makes me feel good." Do you hear the ego in that?

Some men think they could never fall into this ego trap.

EGO NEED CAN LEAD A MAN TO BEHAVE DISHONORABLY. Let me tell you: *it isn't the woman who's so strong; it's the ego that is weak.* Men who decide to leave the path of righteousness in pursuit of other voices rarely make a sudden turn and plunge into error. Instead, they make small, safe departures from what is right, then turn back to evaluate.

They say, "Hmm, I liked that, but I really shouldn't have done it." Remember that once you create a capacity for something, you need more of it to fulfill your desire. So they go out a little farther before coming back. "Oh, boy, that felt good! But I *really* shouldn't be doing it." They evaluate, and they check to see if anyone is watching what they're doing.

Then, seemingly all of sudden, they go out and don't come back. They leave their wives. They abandon everybody and everything—God, family, friends, job. Friends wonder, "What happened? He was such a fine young man." What happened is that the infidelity started slowly; he indulged in it to meet his ego needs, until he was overcome by it.

Some of you have also been quietly testing infidelity. I warn you, just as Paul warned: there is only one way for you to keep your sexuality in order. I know you think I'm going to say prayer. It's not prayer. Paul said, *"It is God's will that you...should avoid sexual immorality; that each of you should learn to control his own body in a way that is holy and honorable"* (1 Thess. 4:3–4).

How can you avoid the trap of ego need? *"Each of you should learn to control his own body."* That is how you keep your life straight. Paul didn't say, "Go to prayer meetings," or "Bind the power of lust." You don't bind lust. God simply says, "Control yourself."

I'll bet you wish there was an easy way out of this thing. You thought I was going to give you some magic answers to control your lust and your passion for sex. They're aren't any easy answers. The answer is: behave yourself. End of discussion. Don't let a woman take advantage of you—and make sure you don't take advantage of a woman's feelings for you.

We shouldn't think we are so spiritual that we're untouchable. Whether you are married or single, when you are tempted to be sexually immoral, run away! Start praying. Avoid contact with the woman. Why? You are living in a body that is designed with complex chemicals and hormones that respond to stimuli from what you see and hear.

Remember that ego need feeds the soul first—even though it leads to bodily sin. Be careful how you respond to a woman's praise and attention. If it is starting to lead to inappropriate attraction, you know you need to back off.

Your ego need must be met in God and what He says about your value to Him. Read and meditate on this remarkable verse to realize your worth in God:

> What is man that you are mindful of him, the son of man that you care for him? You made him a little lower than the heavenly beings and crowned him with glory and honor. You made him ruler over the works of your hands; you put everything under his feet. (Ps. 8:4–6)

YOUR PAST IS NOT YOUR FUTURE

No matter what your sexual past has been, you can receive forgiveness and freedom by coming to Christ, repenting of your sin and wrong ways of thinking, and receiving His love and wholeness. Then you can begin to live out His plan for your sexuality. You will become a true light, illuminating God's ways in the sexual darkness and confusion of our times.

PRINCIPLES

1. Most of us have learned about sexuality from faulty sources instead of from God's Word.

2. The church and the family have often given the impression that sex is unholy and should not be discussed.

3. God designed men and women as sexual beings. He created sex and said that it is *"very good."* (See Genesis 1:31.)

4. God is negative only about the misuse of sex.

5. The Bible uses sexual union in marriage as a metaphor for the intimacy and unity of Christ and His bride, the church.

6. God designed sex within marriage for these reasons: (1) to procreate the human race, (2) to seal a blood covenant between two humans, and (3) to allow sex to be enjoyed to its maximum potential without repercussions.

7. God wants us to enjoy sex so much that He has told us what its safe boundaries are. The primary boundary is the marriage covenant.

8. The body is not meant for immorality. This is one of God's sexual laws, which He has given us for our good.

9. God's design is male and female; not male and male, or female and female. We can know that homosexuality is not God's plan because it does not fit His design.

10. Sex is a physical sign of a spiritual act—the giving of oneself completely to another and for another.

11. Sex was given by God to help express love, not create it.

12. The sexual traps of men are (1) misunderstanding the sexual difference between males and females; (2) the voice of pleasure; (3) the lure of romanticism; (4) the desire for extramarital relationships; and (5) ego need.

10

MALE-FEMALE DIFFERENCES

UNTIL THE MALE RECOGNIZES THE FEMALE'S GOD-GIVEN
STRENGTHS, HE WILL BE WEAK IN THOSE AREAS,
BECAUSE SHE IS DESIGNED TO SUPPLY WHAT HE LACKS.

G od created men and women with perfectly complementary designs. The male is perfect for the female,
and the female is perfect for the male. It is when
men and women expect each other to think, react, and behave in the same ways—that is, when they don't know or
appreciate their God-given differences—that they experience
conflict. Yet when they understand and value each other's
purposes, they can have rewarding relationships, and they
can blend their unique designs harmoniously for God's glory.

One of the greatest problems I've seen while counseling
couples is that husbands and wives don't realize that the
needs of their spouses are different from their own. Remember the principle that purpose deter-
mines nature, and nature determines
needs? If a woman wants to help a
man fulfill his purpose, she must
learn his nature, how he functions,
and what his needs are. She can't
give him what *she* needs, because his
needs are often different from hers. Consider this illustration: you fill up your car's gas tank with gasoline so that it
will run. However, you don't pour gasoline on your plants to
make them grow. Each entity needs to be given what is appropriate for its own nature and needs. The same principle
holds true for males and females.

MALES AND FEMALES HAVE PERFECTLY COMPLEMENTARY DESIGNS.

Sometimes I hear men say, "I don't need a woman."
These men fail to realize that women were designed to benefit them. Recall that when God created the world, He said

that everything was good except for one thing: *"It is not good for the man to be alone. I will make a helper **suitable** for him"* (Gen. 2:18, emphasis added). When God created man's helper, He made her as strong as the man, so that she can help him. We have to appreciate the fact that males and females have different strengths, and that each can't fully function without the other. There are some strengths that God has given the female that the male does not possess. Until he recognizes the strengths God has placed within the female, he will be weak in those areas, because she was designed to supply what he lacks.

THE DISTINCT NATURES OF MEN AND WOMEN

In this chapter, we'll explore the major differences between men and women in the way they think, act, and respond, so we can better meet one another's needs and work cooperatively to fulfill God's purposes. Again, these differences are not right or wrong, better or worse; they are just *different*. Keep in mind also that these are general tendencies.

THE NEED FOR RESPECT LIES AT THE CORE OF A MAN'S SELF-ESTEEM.

Some of these qualities may be manifested in either males or females, depending on how God has gifted them to fulfill their individual purposes.

1. DIFFERENCES IN PRIMARY NEEDS

The primary needs of males are (1) respect, (2) recreational companionship, and (3) sex. The primary needs of females are (1) love, (2) conversation, and (3) affection.

THE MALE'S NEED FOR RESPECT

A man doesn't just desire respect, he needs it. It is part of his nature as leader, protector, and provider. The need for respect is at the core of his self-esteem, and it affects every other area of his life. More than anyone else, a wife can meet her husband's need for admiration and respect by understanding his value and achievements. She needs to remind him of his capabilities and help him to maintain his self-confidence. She should be proud of her husband, not out of duty, but as an expression of sincere admiration for the man with whom she has chosen to share her life.

A single man needs respect as much as a married man does. He needs the sisterly affirmation of female relatives and friends if he is to feel fulfilled as a man.

THE FEMALE'S NEED FOR LOVE

God created the female so the male would have someone with whom to share earthly love. To love means to cherish and to care for. Because she was created for the purpose of receiving love, a woman doesn't just desire love, she truly requires it. As much as a man needs to *know* that he is respected, a woman needs to *feel* that she is loved. A woman wants to feel that she is important and special to her husband. When a man spends time with a woman, it makes her feel cherished because she knows she comes first in his life. She feels cared for when he goes out of his way to make sure she has everything she needs.

RECEIVING LOVE IS A WOMAN'S GREATEST NEED.

If a woman is single, receiving love is still her greatest need. Male relatives and friends can meet her need by showing brotherly love through acts of kindness, companionship, and assistance during life's difficulties.

God affirmed these primary needs in Ephesians 5:33: *"Each one of you* [husbands] *also must love his wife as he loves himself, and the wife must respect her husband."*

THE MALE'S NEED FOR RECREATIONAL COMPANIONSHIP

It is a man's competitive or "territorial" nature that leads to his need for recreational companionship. He needs to be involved in challenging activities, and although he likes to win, he also desires to share these experiences with others. Nothing blesses a man more than when a woman is involved in his favorite recreation. If a wife participates in what her husband enjoys doing—playing tennis, visiting historical landmarks, playing an instrument, or designing computer programs, for example—and lets him tell her all about them, she can strengthen her relationship with him. He will feel good that she is involved with him in his interests. When a couple shares important aspects of their lives with one another, they build understanding, companionship, and intimacy in their marriage.

THE FEMALE'S NEED FOR CONVERSATION

Because males have a leadership mindset, sometimes their conversations with their wives amount to instructions rather than a give-and-take dialogue. A woman desires to have a man talk *with* her, not *at* her.

Some men say, "What am I going to talk about with my wife?" They don't realize that a woman has a need to express herself and therefore has much within her that she wants to share. The man can fulfill a woman's need for intimate conversation by continually making a point to communicate with her. To truly meet her need, he should talk with her at the *feeling* level and not just the knowledge and information level. She needs him to listen to her attitudes about the events of her day with sensitivity, interest, and concern, resisting the impulse to offer solutions. Instead, he should offer his full attention and understanding. A man should conduct his end of the conversation with courtesy and openness, telling her what he really thinks and feels.

A male needs to share his interests, and a female needs conversation: these related needs can be a wonderful bridge of communication between men and women.

THE MALE'S NEED FOR SEX

As we saw in the previous chapter, the male is almost always ready sexually. A man's need for sex is one of the strongest needs imaginable. It is an aspect of his makeup that gives him great fulfillment. Therefore, it is important for a woman to be sensitive to her husband's need for sex.

Sometimes, a woman sees a man's sexual energy as animalistic and thoughtless. If his approach is too abrupt or too aggressive, she may tell him to leave her alone. There are also times when she is not ready for sexual relations because of her cycle, so she will put him off. In these situations, the man may interpret her refusals as disinterest or disrespect, instead of recognizing the underlying reasons behind them.

On the other hand, some women pay more attention to church activities than they do to their husbands. In a sense, they neglect their husbands' sexual needs because they claim they are too busy serving God. Some women may even think it is not "spiritual" for them to engage in physical relations—perhaps because of the way they were brought up. These views are erroneous and can be a damaging witness to a husband. Sex was part of God's original design for humanity, and it is a holy thing between a husband and wife.

Men and women must balance having their own needs fulfilled with showing consideration for one another. The Bible says that husbands and wives are to fulfill one another's sexual needs (1 Cor. 7:3–5). It also says that a husband is to be sensitive to his wife's overall needs, treating her with consideration and respect. (See 1 Peter 3:7.)

THE FEMALE'S NEED FOR AFFECTION

While one of the male's primary needs is sex, one of the female's primary needs is affection. If these two interrelated needs are not lovingly understood and balanced, they can cause some of the worst conflicts in a marriage.

The woman's natural focus is on the sensory, intuitive, and emotional realms of life, and this is why she has a corresponding need for affection. She needs an atmosphere of affection in order to feel loved and fulfilled.

Men and women need to understand that *affection creates the environment for sexual union* in marriage, while *sex is the event.* Most men don't realize this, so they immediately go after the event. They don't know what it means to create an environment of affection. Instead, they focus only on their own needs. Yet affection is something the man has to initiate. If a man is not sure how to be affectionate, he should sit down with his wife and ask her— gently and sincerely.

AFFECTION CREATES THE ENVIRONMENT FOR MARITAL UNION.

Affection is the environment in which to grow a wonderful marriage. Giving affection to a woman means appealing to that which makes her an emotional being. Sometimes a woman just wants her husband to sit with her, hold her hand, and talk with her. Her need can also be met by plenty of hugs and kisses; a steady flow of words, cards, and flowers; common courtesies; and meaningful gifts that show the man is thinking of her—that he esteems her and values her presence in his life.

2. DIFFERENCES IN THINKING AND PROCESSING

Another difference between men and women is that the male is naturally a "logical thinker," whereas the female is naturally an "emotional feeler." A male's first reaction will be a thinking one, but he will also feel. A female's first reaction will be an emotional one, followed by a thinking one. There is a physiological explanation for these tendencies.

Fewer nerves connect the two hemispheres of the male's brain compared to a woman's brain, so that the logical and emotional sides are not as closely related as they are for women. Because of this, a male basically needs to "shift gears" to move from his dominant logical side to his emotional side. This is why men often think in terms of facts and in a linear fashion. They think like a straight line—the shortest distance between two points—which gives them the ability to see the goal (the vision) and to focus their energies on reaching it in the most straightforward and direct way.

Men often dismiss women as emotional or illogical. They don't understand how women are made and the perspective they provide on life. The neural pathways between the left and right hemispheres of a woman's brain (both the logical and the emotional sides) are intact. This is why women are able to do multiple tasks at the same time, rather than having to focus on just one. Women tend to think more like a grid than a straight line. A woman's brain is designed to pick up many details that men don't "see," things that go beyond mere facts, such as the personalities, motivations, and feelings of both herself and others. She can perceive, analyze, evaluate, and see relationships between things all at the same time, like x, y, and z coordinates on a grid track a multiple of factors at the same time.

The woman can help the man see aspects of life, which, if overlooked or ignored, can become detours or potholes preventing him from reaching his goal or from reaching it as quickly as he might have. Her peripheral vision keeps him from being blindsided as he single-mindedly pursues his goals and objectives. On the other hand, the man's linear thinking helps the woman not to become so enmeshed in the many layers of her multi-dimensional thinking and emotions that she loses sight of the goal and never reaches it. Instead of dismissing each another as "unfeeling" or "emotional," men and woman need to appreciate their unique perspectives, which can greatly benefit one another.

3. DIFFERENCES IN SPEAKING AND HEARING LANGUAGE

THE SPOKEN WORD

When a male speaks, it is generally an expression of what he is *thinking*. When a female speaks, it is usually an expression of what she is *feeling*. They are communicating two completely different types of information.

Women often don't understand how very hard it is for men to express their feelings. It's very important for a woman not to come to any firm conclusions about a man's motivation for what he's saying until she discovers what he's feeling. There are many men who are feeling emotions that they have difficulty verbalizing. A woman needs to learn to create an environment that

A MAN SAYS WHAT HE THINKS. A WOMAN SAYS WHAT SHE FEELS.

will enable a man to tell her what he is feeling. When she works through his thinking, she will find out what he is feeling—and she will discover that what he's feeling is often very different from what he's been saying.

In contrast, a woman doesn't always tell a man what she's thinking. If she becomes emotional, he needs to be patient and work through her emotions to find out what she's thinking. Sometimes, he has to dig deep to find out what is actually on her mind—because what a woman is thinking is often different from what she is saying. This process can take patience on the part of the man, because he wants just the facts and likes to quickly arrive at the bottom line. A woman is thinking on a variety of levels, however, and it takes her longer to process all these details and arrive at a conclusion.

If men and women aren't careful, they will come to the wrong conclusions about each other's true intentions, without knowing what the woman is really thinking or the man is really feeling. This error has caused many people to think that their marriages or relationships aren't working. Once they understand these differences, however, they can exercise patience and endeavor to come to the heart of the matter. Both men and women will experience great satisfaction when they are truly listened to and appreciated.

The Heard Word

When a man listens to spoken language, he considers it a process by which he receives information. However, for the female, it is an emotional experience.

A man will hear a verbal communication and conclude that it is either useful or worthless, true or untrue, logical or illogical. It is all facts and information to him. However, because a woman is an "emotional feeler," she evaluates both the verbal and nonverbal communication she receives and perceives from the world around her. She not only receives thoughts and ideas into her being but also transforms them as she processes them. When a woman receives information, she assesses it both mentally and emotionally *at the same time*. The male generally uses these functions separately. Her emotions are with her all the time she is thinking, and this influences her perspective on the world around her as well as what is communicated to her.

When a man and woman learn that they comprehend the spoken word in distinct ways, they can tailor their communication styles to match the way the other best receives and processes information. This method will bring about improved understanding and eliminate much stress in relationships. A man and woman can also broaden their perspectives by asking the other what he or she thought of various people and circumstances they have both encountered.

4. Differences in Problem-Solving

Men are often like filing cabinets. That is, they make decisions quickly and "file" them away in their minds. Or they put a problem in a mental "to do" folder and go on to other things. They reopen the folder only when they feel ready to deal with it. In contrast, women are generally like computers. Their minds keep going and going, working things through, until a problem is solved.

These approaches to problem-solving are the reason men and women will often react differently to life's difficulties or conflicts in interpersonal relationships. Men tend to be resentful about such things, and it's harder for them to see past their anger. They might just "file away" the problems, as we saw earlier. On the other hand, women are guilt-prone; therefore, they often feel responsible for these situations, whether they have caused them or not. Even if they are angry, they will look within to see what they could have done differently or how they can resolve the situation.

Men and women can eliminate much frustration in their relationships by understanding each other's problem-solving strengths and using them to benefit one another. For instance, a woman can assist a man in resolving a problem with a coworker by talking through the difficulty with him and helping him to recognize the motivations and feelings involved. A man can help a woman come to a decision more quickly by acknowledging her feelings about a situation but also clearly outlining for her the facts and options involved. Taking into consideration both intuitive and factual information will help men and women to make better decisions.

5. DIFFERENCES IN REALIZING GOALS

When it comes to material things, such as a job task, a building project, or financial planning, men want to know the details of how to get there. They like to know what steps they must take to achieve a task. In contrast, women tend to look at overall goals. They think about what they want to accomplish rather than focusing on a step-by-step outline of what needs to be done. While a man will sit down and write out a list of points, a woman might just start doing something to make sure it gets done.

However, when it comes to spiritual or intangible things, the opposite is generally true: males look at overall goals, while females want to know how to get there. These tendencies are why men usually remember the gist of a matter, while women often remember the details and overlook or even misconstrue the gist. Men are interested in the principle, the abstract, the philosophy. They see the general direction they need to go in spiritually, and they head toward it. As long as they know what they believe, they don't always see the need for activities designed to help them arrive at their goal. However, women like to be involved in the process. They will attend prayer meetings and Bible studies, read Christian books, and participate more in the life of the church because it will help them grow spiritually.

Men and women can bring balance to one another in both material and spiritual things by helping each other to keep visions and goals clearly in mind while identifying the steps that are necessary to accomplish them effectively.

6. DIFFERENCES IN PERSONALITY AND SELF-PERCEPTION

A man's job is an extension of his personality, whereas a woman's home is an extension of hers. This difference can cause much conflict in relationships.

For instance, a woman may want her husband to spend time with her at home, whereas he can enjoy working twelve hours a day away from the home because he's cultivating something that is a reflection of who he is. He needs to work in order to feel fulfilled. Remember that when a man loses his job, it can be devastating to his self-esteem because he considers his job to be almost synonymous with himself.

A MAN IDENTIFIES WITH HIS JOB. A WOMAN IDENTIFIES WITH HER HOME.

A woman places high value on her physical surroundings and on creating a home. Men don't understand why women become upset when they put their muddy running shoes on the kitchen table or track sawdust in the living room after it has just been vacuumed. Men are not trying to be inconsiderate; they just don't think in the same terms that women do. Because a woman identifies herself with her home, sometimes she feels as if the sawdust has been tracked on *her*. When the beauty and order of the home is disturbed, it can be unsettling for a woman.

Another aspect to the differences in male and female personality and self-perception is that men's personalities are fairly consistent, while woman are continually changing. Women seek personal growth and development more than men do. They like to redecorate the home, discover new skills, or gain a new outlook. Men are often satisfied to follow the same routines, think in the same patterns—and wear the same suits for twenty years.

Understanding these personality traits is essential, because they involve sensitive areas of our lives, such as who we are and how we perceive ourselves. Men and women can use their knowledge of these differences to build up each another's self-esteem and to give each other latitude when one finds change hard and another looks forward to it.

7. DIFFERENCES IN IDEAS OF SECURITY AND COMFORT

Because men put a strong emphasis on their jobs and are not as emotionally connected to their physical surroundings, they have a tendency to be nomadic as they look for new career opportunities. Conversely, many women have a great need for security and roots. While a move due to a new job seems like an adventure for a man and signals progress in his career, it can be stressful and difficult for his wife, who has to leave family and friends behind for an uncertain future. Women will also change geographic locations for jobs; however, married women are less willing to make a move to advance their own jobs than they are for their husbands' jobs. They are less inclined to want to disrupt the lives of their families, especially when they have children.

On the other hand, when it comes to encountering something new, men tend to stand back and evaluate at first. Women are more ready to accept new experiences, and they participate in them more easily. Let's return to the illustration from a previous chapter of a couple attending a new church. The man will scrutinize the people in a church service, to see if they are genuine and trustworthy. A woman is more likely to take what she sees at face value and become involved more quickly.

Matters involving security and comfort can require great understanding on the part of a spouse. They reflect issues such as fulfillment, trustworthiness, fear, and feelings of instability. When men or women want to make job changes or embark on something new, they should be aware of the possible reactions of their spouses and show kindness and patience as they work through these potential changes to their lives.

TRUE FULFILLMENT

As you can see, males and females perceive the world in very distinct ways, and they react differently to people and circumstances. However, they complement one another perfectly, so that they bring balance to each other's lives. What one fails to see, the another perceives. What one is weak in, the other is strong in.

No one person, and no one gender, can look at the world with complete perspective. Therefore, God has designed things so that when the male-man and the female-man live and work together in unity, they can help one another to have a wiser and richer experience of life. They can be more complete as human beings.

Needs are a built-in component to men and women because of the way they are designed. However, when we focus only on our needs, and when we refuse to be content unless they are immediately met, we bring conflict and unhappiness into our relationships. We stop seeing one another as gifts from God and start resenting one another.

If you want to be blessed, don't focus on your needs but discover what the other person's needs are and seek to fulfill them. This approach will become a double blessing, because consistently meeting the needs of another person will often cause that person to want to fulfill yours. Whenever you are not receiving what you need in a relationship, evaluate whether you have been trying to meet the other person's needs first. Giving to others by satisfying their needs—not demanding to have our own needs satisfied—will bring true fulfillment.

PRINCIPLES

1. Men and women have perfectly complementary designs.

2. When men and women don't appreciate their differences, they experience conflict. When they value each other's purposes, they can have rewarding relationships and blend their unique designs harmoniously for God's glory.

3. Until the male recognizes the strengths God has placed within the female, he will be weak in those areas, because she is designed to supply what he lacks.

4. The primary needs of males are (1) respect, (2) recreational companionship, and (3) sex. The primary needs of females are (1) love, (2) conversation, and (3) affection.

5. A male is naturally a "logical thinker," while a female is naturally an "emotional feeler."

6. A male generally expresses what he's *thinking*. A female usually expresses what she's *feeling*. To a male, listening to spoken language is a process by which he receives information. For the female, it's an emotional experience.

7. Men are often like filing cabinets: they make quick decisions and mentally file them away, or they create mental "to do" folders, filing away problems until a later time. Women are generally like computers: their minds keep working through problems until they are solved.

8. In material things, men usually want to know the details of how to get there, while women tend to look at the goal. In spiritual things, the opposite is often true.

9. A man's job is an extension of his personality, while a woman's home is an extension of hers. A man's personality is fairly consistent, while a woman's is continually changing.

10. Men are nomadic, while women need security and roots.

11. When encountering something new, men tend to stand back and evaluate. Women are more ready to accept new experiences, and they participate in them more easily.

11

HOW TO BE A
GOOD FATHER

A FATHER IS MEANT TO REPRESENT THE FATHERHOOD OF
GOD TO HIS CHILDREN.

N ever before in the history of the world have we been
as much in need of good fathers. When God created
the male and gave him his dominion assignments,
He included the responsibility of cultivating and protecting
his offspring. Yet today, there is a widespread lack of understanding about the nature of fatherhood. Men of all nations
and races lack the skills of good parenting.

Certain men think that their ability to produce a child
makes them a man. Any male can have a baby. Merely
having a child is no guarantee that you are a real man—or
a real father. These men don't know the meaning of being a
covering, protection, and role model for their children.

Many men were never taught what it means to be a good
father, and their own fathers did not provide good examples
for them. The problems we encounter with our parents in the
early years of our lives can be transferred into our own families after we marry, if they have not been resolved. When fathers are a negative influence on their sons, boys grow up
with the wrong concept of marriage and fatherhood. Broken
relationships and families are the result.

In a large number of homes today, fathers are absent,
due to separation, divorce, and the rising number of out-of-
wedlock births. Other fathers live in the home but are absent
from the family for all intents and purposes. They have for-
saken their responsibility as fathers because of career pursuits, indifference, and selfishness, as they put their own
pleasures ahead of their children's welfare. This means that
many children don't have the benefit of a good father.

A Tremendous Calling

Gentlemen, we have a tremendous calling ahead of us. Our task involves changing not only our own perspectives of fatherhood, but also those of our children, especially our sons. We have to communicate to them the standards of God, so that the trend I've just described can be reversed. But we have to start with ourselves. We must discover and put into practice what the Word of God says *about* fathers and *to* fathers. Then we can teach these principles to other men and boys. God's truth about fathers will be the salvation of our communities and nations.

God has always been very specific in His Word about the responsibilities of a father. This role is of particular importance to Him, because fathers are meant to represent Him to their children. The fatherhood of God is indicative of His nature; it is the way **FATHERS** He desires to relate to us. When fathers **REPRESENT** fail to show His love and character to **GOD TO** their sons and daughters, the children's **THEIR** concept of God suffers, affecting their **CHILDREN.** relationships with Him. Now, no earthly father can ever be perfect. Yet God has provided a wealth of instruction on parenting in His Word. When men look to Him, they can fulfill their responsibilities and be meaningful reflections of the fatherhood of God to their children. What, then, does it mean to be a good father?

The Responsibilities of a Father

1. A Good Father Knows the Heavenly Father

A man won't be able to understand what it means to be a good father if he doesn't know His heavenly Father. When Jesus rose from the dead, He made this wonderful statement: *"I am returning to my Father and your Father, to my God and your God"* (John 20:17). Because of Jesus' death and resurrection on our behalf, we can know God not only as our Creator but also as our Father.

A man must also have *faith* in God as His Father—that He will love, protect, and provide for him. Trust and reliance on God is what a father needs to model for his children. The greatest heritage a man can leave his sons and daughters is not money or property, but faith. A house can burn down, or someone can sell or repossess it, but no one can destroy the faith you have instilled in your child. Besides, the child will be able to use his faith to obtain another house, because He has been taught to trust God as his Provider.

In the Bible, you will often see variations on the phrase, *"the God of my father."* (See, for example, Genesis 26:24; 32:9; 2 Chronicles 17:4; Isaiah 38:5.) Men, if you have one goal in life, let it be this: before you die, you will hear your children say, "I serve the God of my father." If they have seen God reflected in you, then you have displayed His life and character to them. In doing so, you have given them a true spiritual heritage.

LET YOUR GOAL BE TO HEAR YOUR CHILDREN SAY, "I SERVE THE GOD OF MY FATHER."

Why did the children of the patriarchs follow the God of their fathers? He kept His promises and took care of them. In Genesis 12:2, God said to Abraham, *"I will make you into a great nation and I will bless you; I will make your name great, and you will be a blessing."* Later, we see how God began to fulfill this promise. Abraham's servant reported,

> *The LORD has blessed my master abundantly, and he has become wealthy. He has given him sheep and cattle, silver and gold, menservants and maidservants, and camels and donkeys. My master's wife Sarah has borne him a son in her old age, and he has given him everything he owns.* (Gen. 24:35)

Abraham's son, Isaac, saw firsthand that the God of His father was real, and he decided, "I'm going to serve my father's God, too." Today, many children are turning away from the true God because their fathers' faith is weak, and therefore they think their fathers' God is also weak. The God whom their fathers serve doesn't seem to be living up to what He's supposed to, so the children are disillusioned.

If you are a father, your children are looking up to you and saying, "Show me God." Your representation of God in the home will likely determine what your children will say in the end. Will they say, "I will serve the God of my father"? Or will they say, "The God of my father is not worth serving"? I want my children to see the faithfulness of God displayed in my life. I want them to be able to say, "This God that my father and mother serve does everything He says He will do. My mother said that God was going to do this, and He did it. My father prayed that this would happen, and it happened. This God is real. I will follow the God of my parents because He is faithful."

2. A GOOD FATHER LOVES THE MOTHER OF HIS CHILDREN

The second most important thing a man can do for his children is to love their mother. Many men buy gifts for their children, such as bicycles and computers, when what the children want and need most is to see their fathers truly love their mothers. I think there is nothing more precious than for a child to see his parents being affectionate with one another. I think kids get a feeling of security when they see that.

Showing consideration and respect for your wife is extremely important. Are you demanding and impatient with your spouse, or do you treat her with kindness and understanding? What are you modeling for your children about what it means to be a husband? Children take in everything they see, and your children observe the way you treat your wife much more than you may know. A child will often lose respect for his father if he doesn't see him giving his mother the consideration and love she deserves.

Many men don't realize that their treatment of their wives affects not only how their children see them, but also how God views them. If a husband doesn't treat his wife with respect, his very prayers may be hindered:

> *Husbands, in the same way be considerate as you live with your wives, and treat them with respect...so that nothing will hinder your prayers.* (1 Pet. 3:7)

When you love the mother of your children, you bring peace and happiness into your home, and you teach your children by example what it means to be a real man.

3. A GOOD FATHER LOVES HIS CHILDREN

Many parents think love means providing their children with clothes, food, and shelter. That's merely a natural and moral duty. Anyone with common sense and a little bit of conscience would buy food. Love is much more than that. There are fathers who pay the rent for their children, but don't go to visit them. There are fathers who buy their children Christmas gifts, but send them with somebody else. Buying things for your kids doesn't necessarily mean you love them. It may mean you feel guilty about not fulfilling your responsibility to them. Some men don't even want to do that. They don't pay child support, so the courts have to deal with them.

LOVE IS NOT BUYING GIFTS. IT IS YOU *BEING* A GIFT.

Love is not buying gifts. Love is *you being a gift*. The Bible tells us that our heavenly Father so loved the world that He became a revelation of that love in Jesus Christ. Therefore, if a man is really a father, he doesn't just send gifts. He sends himself. That's the essence of love.

Love also means correcting, chastening, and reproving your children when they need it. We'll take a closer look at these responsibilities in coming sections. However, let me say here that some children are begging to be corrected, but their fathers don't have any sense to realize it. Some children hate their fathers because they let them do whatever they want. The fathers think the children will do fine on their own. They say, "My child is old enough to handle it," while their children are thinking, "I need help, Daddy! I don't know the right values in life. I don't have standards to judge by. I'm looking to you to give me some guidelines, and you're telling me, 'Decide for yourself.'"

Loving your children means setting standards for them. Life today is very complex and confused. Children need someone who can tell them, "This is the way in which to go." You need to give your children a love that instills eternal values. I've talked to parents who were concerned because their child was wayward. "I don't know what happened. I gave him everything he wanted." That was the problem. You don't give your child everything he wants. You give him what he needs.

There are times when love has to be tough. Some fathers don't have the backbone for that. They are afraid to punish their children, so they leave it up to their wives. The Bible never says the mother is to correct the children; it says the father is to discipline them. Yet how many fathers leave discipline up to the mothers? Some fathers don't punish their children because they want the children to like them. They don't realize the effect this has on their families. The children begin to love their mother more than their father because they know their mother cares enough to correct them. They think, "Daddy doesn't really love me." They may also grow up believing a parent isn't supposed to discipline his children, so they don't become good agents of correction for their own children. If you love your children, you will correct them.

4. A Good Father Is Responsible for His Children

There is a popular idea today that every person should take total responsibility for himself or herself, no matter how young that person is—that a child has "children's rights" that are the same as an adult's. This philosophy teaches that a parent cannot spank a child as a disciplinary measure. If this happens, the child should be able to go to court and get an injunction against his parent for hurting him. It also says a child should also be able to "divorce" his parents.

What the world is saying is that children should be allowed to bring themselves up. This idea is foolish. You don't treat children as adults. Children are children; grown-ups are grown-ups. Sometimes adults act like children. But children are definitely not adults and shouldn't be treated as if they were. **WHO IS REALLY RAISING YOUR CHILDREN?** Parents have a responsibility before God to raise their children. God does not leave the care and upbringing of your children to themselves or to society. He leaves it to you.

How much time do you spend with your children? Who is really bringing them up? Perhaps you and your wife leave for work early in the morning and don't return until late in the evening. You don't see much of your children. Someone else has brought them up all day. Realize that everything that person represents goes into your children. They will learn their views of God, their concept of themselves, and their philosophy of life from their caretaker. You need to be careful whom you allow to watch your children.

To be responsible for your children, you must make time for them. They should not be considered one more item on a "to do" list or one more obstacle to clear out of your way. Many fathers don't really want to take responsibility for their children, because children take time and energy. Therefore, they leave them to fend for themselves. Balancing all of life's demands can be difficult for a father, but your children should be at the top of the list, after your wife.

5. A GOOD FATHER TEACHES AND INSTRUCTS HIS CHILDREN

A father needs to read and study the Word of God so he can teach it to his children. He must know the commands of God. It's impossible to teach something you haven't learned yourself. Remember what God said about Abraham, whom He called His friend?

> *Abraham will surely become a great and powerful nation, and all nations on earth will be blessed through him. For I have chosen him, so that he will direct his children and his household after him to keep the way of the LORD by doing what is right and just.*
> (Gen. 18:18–19)

God made a promise to Abraham and said the fulfillment of the promise was connected to Abraham's teaching his family the Word of God. There's a relationship between the two. God is holding up some fathers' blessings because they aren't loving their children enough to teach them the Word.

In the book of Proverbs, Solomon spoke of the wisdom to be gained from godly instruction:

> *My son, if you accept my words and store up my commands within you, turning your ear to wisdom and applying your heart to understanding, and if you call out*

204

for insight and cry aloud for understanding, and if you look for it as for silver and search for it as for hidden treasure, then you will understand the fear of the LORD and find the knowledge of God. For the LORD gives wisdom, and from his mouth come knowledge and understanding. (Prov. 2:1–6)

When fathers teach their children the commands of God, their children will learn that fathers who know the Word are worth listening to. Proverbs 1:8–9 says, *"Listen, my son, to your father's instruction and do not forsake your mother's teaching. They will be a garland to grace your head and a chain to adorn your neck."* A garland was a crown or wreath given to athletes who won a race. When children receive godly instructions from their fathers, they can win the race that ends in eternal life.

6. A GOOD FATHER TRAINS AND DISCIPLINES HIS CHILDREN

In Hosea 11:3–4, God said,

It was I who taught Ephraim to walk, taking them by the arms; but they did not realize it was I who healed them. I led them with cords of human kindness, with ties of love; I lifted the yoke from their neck and bent down to feed them.

"It was I who taught Ephraim to walk." God was talking about His people. He was saying, "I have always been with you. From the time you were a child, I was working with you. When you fell down, I picked you up. I was training you." That's the spirit of a father. Our heavenly Father takes a personal interest in our training. Likewise, we are to personally train our children.

Proverbs 19:18 says, *"Discipline your son, for in that there is hope; do not be a willing party to his death."* This is serious business. The verse is saying, "Discipline and train a child now because there is hope in that discipline, hope in that training." You are giving hope to your child when you discipline and correct him. You are giving him a value system for his entire life.

The Scripture says if you don't do this, you're a party to your child's death. Now, we use the phrase "a party to" to refer to criminals, don't we? Someone commits a murder, and another person is there assisting. Or someone robs a store, and another person drives the getaway car. The second person is called a party to the crime, which means that he or she is just as guilty as the one who committed the wrong. So the Scripture is saying that if you don't correct or discipline your child when he needs it, then when he goes bad, you are responsible.

Proverbs 29:15 says, *"A child left to himself disgraces his mother."* Check out the children in the reform schools. Check out the inmates in the prisons. Look at the people living on the streets. Many of them were left to themselves as children, with no one to teach them character and values.

My heart goes out to single parents who have to fill the roles of both father and mother. I want to say to you: don't let your children train you. You may not know everything in life, but you know more than they do. And that's enough for you to be in charge. I don't care how old they are, when you're paying the mortgage, when you're providing for them, you make the rules. If they disobey the rules, you have to make sure they experience the consequences.

"Train up a child in the way he should go: and when he is old, he will not depart from it" (Prov. 22:6 KJV). The word for **"train"** in this verse is the same word that is used for conditioning. The Bible is saying, "Condition your child in the way he should go." Why? He can't condition himself. He was born with a rebellious spirit. You don't have to teach your children to swear, lie, steal, commit adultery, or have bitterness and hatred. It's already in them. If you don't condition them, they will naturally become wayward. You have to train them.

YOU MAY NOT KNOW EVERYTHING, BUT YOU KNOW MORE THAN YOUR CHILDREN DO.

The things children learn from their parents never leave them. I still retain what my father and mother taught me. Do you know that the same temptations that come to any young man came to me? What kept me on an even keel is the values and morals that were instilled in me. There were situations where, if it wasn't for the training of my parents, I would have gone under. The only thing that kept me safe was the character I learned from their teaching and correction. I love my parents because they disciplined me.

Hebrews 12:7 tells us the benefits of discipline:

Endure hardship as discipline; God is treating you as sons. For what son is not disciplined by his father? If you are not disciplined (and everyone undergoes discipline), then you are illegitimate children and not true sons. Moreover, we have all had human fathers who disciplined us and we respected them for it. How much more should we submit to the Father of our spirits and live! Our fathers disciplined us for a little while as they thought best; but God disciplines us for our good, that we may share in his holiness. No discipline seems pleasant at the time, but painful. Later on, however, it produces a harvest of righteousness and peace for those who have been trained by it.

"No discipline seems pleasant at the time, but painful. Later on, however, it produces a harvest of righteousness and peace for those who have been trained by it." If you train your children, they will grow up to know God's ways and to have peace in their hearts.

The King James Version uses the word *"chastening"* instead of *"discipline."* The word *chasten* means "to correct," "to reprove," or "to discipline." Some children are punished but not corrected. Parents sometimes confuse the two. Your children need discipline. To discipline means to instill moral and mental character, to give values to a person. You don't give values just by punishing. You give values by correcting.

My parents had a wonderful way of sitting me down and saying, "Now, here is why we punished you." They didn't just punish me; they corrected me. They said, "If you keep this up, this will happen," and "If you keep this kind of company, this will be the result." Disciplining your children may be somewhat painful for both you and your children at times, but the results will be positive and healthy.

7. A GOOD FATHER ENCOURAGES HIS CHILDREN

First Thessalonians 2:11–12 says, *"For you know that we dealt with each of you as a father deals with his own children, encouraging, comforting and urging* [or warning] *you to live lives worthy of God, who calls you into his kingdom and glory."* This passage gives us three additional responsibilities of a good father: encouraging, comforting, and warning.

First, children need encouragement. Some children never hear an encouraging word from their fathers. Do you hear how some fathers talk to their children? They act as if the children can't do anything right. A ten-year-old boy is washing the dishes. His father comes in and says, "Can't you clean dishes better than this?" The little guy is at least trying. So encourage him. Maybe he leaves a little soap on the stove or counter. Don't look at what he left; look at what he cleaned up. Encourage him.

Maybe your child can't read quite as fast as you did when you were her age. Don't criticize her. Encourage her. Some children are really trying. Sometimes a child will try to help out with the chores and will unintentionally break something. His parent will run into the room and yell, "What are you doing?" He gets a lecture. So he goes to his room with a broken heart, a depressed spirit, and a hurt ego. He thinks, "I'm not going to help ever again!" Some parents don't see their child's intention. They see only their own anger and frustration.

SOME CHILDREN NEVER HEAR AN ENCOURAGING WORD FROM THEIR FATHERS.

I'll never forget something that happened when I was still a young Christian. My sister was a little girl, and I was painting a picture of her. It was almost finished, and it had turned out really beautifully. I left the painting on the easel, with the paints out, and walked away for a moment. When I came back, I saw my sister putting red paint all over my picture. She was singing and having a great time. I wanted to slap her, but I took a firm grip on my impatience. In that moment, the Holy Spirit spoke to me, saying, "Don't look at what she did. Look at what she was trying to do." You

208

wouldn't believe what I did. I said, "Finish it." Guess what? Art became her favorite subject in school. She didn't mean to destroy my painting. She was just trying to paint.

Fathers need to encourage their children in what they are *trying* to do, even though it's not perfect. Maybe your son didn't receive an A in class, but at least he went to class. There are some kids who skip their classes. The teacher knows that at least your child tried. So correct and instruct your child with patience, and encourage his or her efforts.

8. A Good Father Comforts His Children

Next, children need comforting. You encourage them when they're doing something positive, and when you want them to improve in something. But there will be times when they become discouraged, hurt, confused, or disillusioned. That is when they need comfort.

How can you comfort your children? By letting them know they are loved, even when they make mistakes or don't live up to your expectations. By listening to their struggles and problems with kindness and understanding. By giving them warm embraces and loving words when they are sad.

To be a comforter, you have to be accessible to your children. You have to know what's going on in their lives so you can know when they're going through struggles and loneliness. Children will be comforted to know you're available to them and that you make it a point to spend time with them. Your comfort will also help them to know that their heavenly Father is a Comforter, just as He is described in His Word: *"the Father of compassion and the God of all comfort, who comforts us in all our troubles"* (2 Cor. 1:3–4).

9. A Good Father Warns His Children

Fathers are also to urge or warn their children to live righteously. Yet how many fathers confuse warning with threatening? "I'm going to kill you if you don't stop that!" Some fathers don't have any kind of tact, because they don't know any better. A child interprets a warning as love, but sees a threat as hate.

The Bible says to warn children *"to live lives worthy of God"* (1 Thess. 2:12). This verse is talking about spiritual warning. It is a father's responsibility to warn his children of the consequences of rejecting God. "Son, there is an eternal hell. I warn you, whatever you sow on earth, you're going to reap in the next life." "Daughter, I warn you that whatever you become involved in will follow you in your memory forever." That's spiritual warning.

Many fathers warn their children, but their children don't listen to them because they aren't setting a godly example. If you are walking in God's ways when you warn your children, they will come to respect the God of their father. They will say, "If I obey my father, then I'm obeying my God. I know that my father knows what is best because I see God working in his life. I'll obey my father because I want Him to work in my life, too."

Some of you may not live with your children. Maybe you are divorced, and your children live in another state or country. I suggest that you write them letters. It's amazing what you can communicate through a letter. You can put things in writing that you find hard to verbalize. Establish a loving relationship with your children through letters, so that you will have their respect when you want to warn them about spiritual realities. Then when you are no longer here, they will remember, "My father told me about God. He wasn't always the best daddy all those years. But before he died, in those latter years, he told me about God. He left me enough that I know that he loves me beyond the grave." Warn your children. It's your responsibility.

10. A Good Father Does Not Provoke His Children

Last, fathers need to be careful not to provoke their children. The Bible says, *"Fathers, do not exasperate your children"* (Eph. 6:4), or *"Do not provoke your children to anger"* (NAS). What are fathers to do instead? *"Bring them up in the training and instruction of the Lord"* (v. 4).

Fathers have a way of provoking their children by impatience or harshness. Yet sometimes *provocation* means more than we normally think of in connection with the word. Notice that the above verse refers to *"training"* and *"instruction"* as the opposites of provocation: "Don't provoke, but train. Don't provoke, but instruct."

Provocation can mean neglect. When you neglect your children, you incite them to despise you. Some fathers have no sensitivity to their children's needs, so the children become exasperated, provoked. They end up with inferiority complexes and undeveloped personalities, because their fathers didn't show them the love and kindness of God.

WHAT WILL YOUR LEGACY BE?

My prayer is that every father or potential father reading this book will take a look at his life and ask himself, "What can I leave my children?"

Do you want to leave them a house? Fine. However, that doesn't mean you will leave them a home. Do you want to leave them a car? Good. But that doesn't mean you will have taught them to be responsible enough to take care of it. Do you want to leave them some books? Wonderful. Yet that doesn't mean you're going to leave them with the interest to read them. Values are transmitted by example, not talk. Morals are transmitted by personification, not lectures.

Proverbs 17:6 says, *"Parents are the pride of their children."* I think the greatest thing a father could hear his child say is, "That's my daddy. I'm proud of him. He's the best father." Will your children be able to say of you, "The pride of my life is my father"? or "I want to be just like my father"?

When your children want to be like you, they want to be like God, whom you represent. Ephesians 5:1 says, *"Be imitators of God, therefore, as dearly loved children."* As you imitate your heavenly Father, your children will imitate you and reflect the character and life of their Creator. That is what the dominion assignment of fatherhood is all about.

PRINCIPLES

A good father—

1. Knows the heavenly Father and represents God to his children.
2. Loves the mother of his children.
3. Loves his children.
4. Is responsible for his children.
5. Teaches and instructs his children.
6. Trains and disciplines his children.
7. Encourages his children.
8. Comforts his children.
9. Warns his children.
10. Does not provoke his children.
11. Leaves a strong spiritual legacy for his children.

12

KEYS TO BECOMING
A REAL MAN

GOD'S PURPOSES SHOULD SATURATE AND OVERFLOW
A MAN'S LIFE.

You are *born* a male, but you have to *become* a man. This means that someone could actually grow up to be just an old male, never living as a real man. In this book, we've explored how a male can be transformed into the man God purposed when He created the world. Becoming God's man is the only way a male can live a satisfying and meaningful life, because His purpose is the key to fulfillment.

To become a real man, a male needs to understand that God's purposes must permeate his entire life so they can overflow into the lives of others. When God gave man dominion over the earth, He was saying, "I am giving you stewardship over creation. Take care of it, so that it will always be a reflection of My character and purposes." To be a steward means to be given a trust over what belongs to someone else. A man is responsible for living out God's purposes in the world and enabling others to do so, also.

The following are ten keys to becoming a real man that incorporate the themes, truths, and principles we've learned throughout this book—all of which come down to a stewardship of the lives and resources with which God has entrusted us. Read and reread these keys until the true meaning of what it means to be a man permeates your understanding, and God's presence and purposes overflow from your life to the world around you.

KEY #1
A REAL MAN DESIRES AND LOVES GOD AND HIS PRESENCE

A real man seeks intimate communion with God by remaining continually in His presence. He loves to worship the

One who created and redeemed him. A real man's spiritual priorities take precedence over his physical and temporal ones. In Luke 4:3, the devil tempted Jesus with a physical need. *"If you are the Son of God, tell this stone to become bread."* Jesus replied, in essence, "No, you don't understand. I have My priorities sorted out. I would rather be in God's presence than satisfy any temporal hunger." (See verse 4.) A real man is clear about what his priorities are.

KEY #2
A REAL MAN SEEKS TO RESTORE GOD'S IMAGE IN HIMSELF

A real man wants to be spiritually renewed so that the fullness of God's image and likeness is restored to his life. He seeks to return to the original plan that God intended when He first made man. This plan is that males and females would reflect the nature of God, who is Spirit, while living as physical beings on the earth. A real man is not deceived by or enamored with counterfeit images of manhood, such as the popular culture presents. A real man wants to be what he was created to be. He wants to be like his Father God.

KEY #3
A REAL MAN ASPIRES TO WORK AND TO DEVELOP HIS GIFTS AND TALENTS

After God placed Adam in His presence, He gave him work. Jesus, the Second Adam, seemed to have two favorite words that reflected God's purposes for man. One was *Father.* He was always talking about His Father in heaven and seeking His presence in prayer. The other was *work.* For example, consider these statements of Jesus: *"My food is to do the will of Him who sent Me, and to finish His work"* (John 4:34 NKJV). *"My Father is always at his work to this very day, and I, too, am working"* (John 5:17). *"As long as it is day, we must do the work of him who sent me. Night is coming, when no one can work"* (John 9:4). *"I have brought you glory on earth by completing the work you gave me to do"* (John 17:4).

Jesus was intent on doing His Father's work to completion. A real man aspires to do the work of God the Father, while developing and using the gifts and talents God has given him. He isn't lazy; he has a vision for his life, and he is willing to work to fulfill it. In God's economy, a man who works and makes mistakes is better than a man who doesn't do anything.

A real man's motivation for work is to fulfill the purposes for which he was created. Jesus said, *"I tell you the truth, you are looking for me, not because you saw miraculous signs but because you ate the loaves and had your fill. Do not work for food that spoils, but for food that endures to eternal life, which the Son of Man will give you"* (John 6:26–27). In other words, there's a higher reason to work. Don't work just to pay bills. Don't work just to buy food. Understand the true nature of work. In the Garden, there was no supervisor, no one to hand out paychecks. Work was given to Adam because it was a natural part of his being. Through work, he fulfilled his purpose as a man.

Matthew 25:16, which comes from the parable of the talents, is a powerful verse: *"The man who had received the five talents went at once and put his money to work and gained five more."* How did the man gain more money? He put his original money to work, and the money multiplied. God wants us to go to work to multiply His kingdom on earth.

KEY #4

A REAL MAN HONORS HIS MARRIAGE AND FAMILY ABOVE PERSONAL INTEREST

Jesus' first miracle was at a wedding (John 2:1–11). In this way, His ministry was introduced to the world as one that supports the family. Jesus is a family Man. His number one desire right now is to be married to His bride, the church. The books of Ephesians and Colossians say that the Holy Spirit is our seal of salvation. Like an engagement ring, the Spirit is our promise that we're going to be married to our Bridegroom, Jesus. The book of Revelation says that Jesus is waiting for His bride. After He returns to earth for us, we will be with Him at the Marriage Supper of the Lamb. We will be consummated with Christ.

Jesus loves His betrothed. He is a family man, and He takes care of His bride. The Bible says that He gave His life for her. He washes her *"by the washing with water through the word"* (Eph. 5:26). A man is to love his wife *"just as Christ loved the church and gave himself up for her....Husbands ought to love their wives as their own bodies"* (vv. 25, 28). A real man protects and takes care of his wife and family, looking out for their needs before his own. A few real men who truly understood this truth and endeavored to live it out could set a standard for entire nations.

KEY #5
A REAL MAN ENDEAVORS TO LEARN, LIVE, AND TEACH GOD'S WORD AND PRINCIPLES

In Genesis 2:15–17, God commanded the first man to keep His word, saying that if he disobeyed it, he would die. In this act, He established the principle that *"man does not live on bread alone, but on every word that comes from the mouth of God"* (Matt. 4:4).

A real man is a man of principles. He realizes that his spirit must be nourished by the Word of God or his spiritual health will decline. God's Word is the precept by which he lives. Because he is a responsible leader, he is also committed to teaching the Scriptures to his family.

A real man allows the Word to transform his life so that he can represent God's will on earth, thus spreading the Garden of God's presence to a world living in the darkness of sin and separation from God:

> *Do everything without complaining or arguing, so that you may become blameless and pure, children of God without fault in a crooked and depraved generation, in which you shine like stars in the universe as you hold out the word of life.*　　　　　(Phil. 2:14–16)

KEY #6
A REAL MAN DEMONSTRATES FAITH AND INSPIRES IT IN OTHERS

When you return to your original image as a man, you become a person who makes people believe that anything is possible. Can you think of Jesus as being anything less than that? He was the only One in history who said, *"Nothing is impossible with God"* (Luke 1:37). What He said is so high that only God could have said it.

Jesus not only said it, but He also believed it. That's why the beggar, the prostitute, and the religious man all kept coming to Him. He made them believe nothing was impossible. A real man has a spirit of faith and inspires others.

Wouldn't you like to be around someone who says, "You can do it. I know things are tough, but you're going to make it," and "Everyone fails once in a while. Get back up and try again"? Even in the darkest hour, a real man believes that there's a way out. He will tell you a thousand times, "Get up again; you can do it." Counterfeit men have no faith. They say things like, "You're talking about starting a business? You'd better hang on to that secure job you have." A real man knows that no job can give a person true security, so he puts his faith in God and trusts His leading. Sometimes a real man might be scared, but he won't worry, because he trusts in God to finish the work He started. Faith is believing in what God said, not in what you see. That's the faith of a real man.

KEY #7
A REAL MAN IS COMMITTED TO CULTIVATING OTHERS TO BE THE BEST THEY CAN BE

A real man endeavors to encourage others to reflect the image and creativity of God in all they are and do—spiritually, emotionally, psychologically, and physically. He prays for wisdom and guidance on how to cultivate his wife and children so they can mature in Christ and become all that God has created them to be. He encourages his family in their gifts and talents while helping them develop in any way he can. As a cultivator, he delights in seeing these gifts unfold in their lives, just as God delights in seeing us use our abilities for His glory.

KEY #8
A REAL MAN LOVES COMPASSION, MERCY, AND JUSTICE

A real man exercises compassion, mercy, and justice. Through them, he shows true strength and brings the kingdom of God to others.

Compassion is passion that is aimed at setting people free. Every time Jesus had compassion, He was about to fix something. If people were hungry, He had compassion and fed them. If they were *"like sheep without a shepherd"* (Matt. 9:36), He had compassion and said, "I am the Good Shepherd; I'll lead you." (See John 10:11–15.) To show compassion means to apply one's strength to meet people's needs.

Mercy is not treating a person as he deserves when he has committed a wrong against you. God has extended mercy to us in salvation. *"But God demonstrates his own love for us in this: while we were still sinners, Christ died for us"* (Rom. 5:8). As His representatives on earth, He wants us to show mercy, also. We are not to seek revenge against others, but are to freely forgive them and do everything we can to lead them to Christ. *"We are therefore Christ's ambassadors, as though God were making his appeal through us. We implore you on Christ's behalf: be reconciled to God"* (2 Cor. 5:20).

Justice means doing what is right by others. God hates injustice. A real man reflects His nature and character by following His command to *"act justly and to love mercy and to walk humbly with your God"* (Mic. 6:8).

KEY #9
A REAL MAN IS FAITHFUL AND LOYAL TO THE KINGDOM OF GOD AND HIS MISSION, THE CHURCH

In Matthew 6:33, Jesus reduced life to one thing: *"Seek first his kingdom and his righteousness, and all these things will be given to you as well."* He was saying, in effect, "Look, all of you are talking about your mortgages, cars, lands, clothing, food, drink, and everything else. You have your priorities confused. Seek first the kingdom of God."

A real man has a passion to see the kingdom of God established in his country. Sinners make him sad. Broken lives depress him. People who don't know Christ concern him. A real man rejoices when people are delivered from the devil. The Bible says that Jesus sent out His disciples with the authority to cast out demons, heal the sick, and raise the dead. (See Luke 10:1–24.) When they came back, what did

Jesus do? The Bible says He was *"full of joy"* (Luke 10:21). In the Greek, the word this phrase comes from means to "jump for joy," or "be exceedingly glad." Jesus began to leap. He was excited about men setting other men free. He said to the disciples, *"Do not rejoice that the spirits submit to you, but rejoice that your names are written in heaven"* (v. 20). In other words, "Don't rejoice that the demons are afraid of you. Rejoice that you are saved. This is what makes Me happy." Real men have the spirit of the Great Commission in their lives: a love for souls and a passion for others to know Christ.

KEY #10
A REAL MAN KEEPS HIMSELF IN GOD

Finally, a real man doesn't take God's presence in His life for granted. He guards his heart and actions so that he can stay close to God and continually reflect His character and ways. He puts the entire weight of his trust in the Lord because he knows that God is *"able to keep* [him] *from falling and to present* [him] *before his glorious presence without fault and with great joy"* (Jude 24).

A FINAL WORD

Communities and nations will be transformed when men return to God and His purposes for them. God is looking for those who will dedicate themselves to standing *"in the gap on behalf of the land"* (Ezek. 22:30). He wants to bring His life-changing power to broken marriages, damaged families, shattered societies, and individual men, women, and children who need reconciliation with God and a restoration of His purposes for them. But He's waiting for men like you. Real men who will commit themselves to fulfilling their dominion purpose of spreading God's presence throughout the whole world. I pray that people will be able to look at your life and say, "Now I know what a real man looks like," as they are transformed by God's presence in you.

A WORD TO MEN OF
THIRD-WORLD NATIONS

The 6.7 billion people who call this planet home are divided into various categories. The largest sector has become identified as Third-World nations. The term *Third World* is one that is despised and resented by many who interpret it to mean inferior, poor, undeveloped, and backward. This term was coined many years ago by an economist at a G-5 meeting in Geneva as an attempt to define the world in economic terms. The intent was not to degrade any people group but rather to identify nations that fell within a common historical grid that resulted in their having common socioeconomic conditions and other similar characteristics.

Technically speaking, the term was an attempt to describe a grouping of peoples who were not allowed to develop or maximize their true potential because they were victims of colonial oppression or regimes that suppressed the creative and progressive instincts of the masses. The vast majority of them were not allowed to participate or benefit directly from the industrial revolution, but rather were victims of it by being used as human fuel—slaves for the engines of industry. Many of these people are products of slavery, colonization, indentured servitude, or ideological oppression. The group that is known today as *Third World* makes up more than two-thirds of the world's population and comprises every race, color, ethnic background, and nationality. Third-World nations, therefore, include billions of people still struggling to find their place in the global scheme of social, technical, and economic advancement.

The nature of their history—slavery, displacement, social abuse, and cultural emasculation—rendered many of these people without a sense of self-worth or a clear self-concept. Many were torn away from their families, traditions, and culture—abandoned to survive in a world with no definitions to guide them. The impact on the males in these historical tragedies was most dramatic. They were stripped of their human dignity, sense of manhood, masculinity, and understanding of purpose. The results were devastating, as many of these men lost hope, self-esteem, and meaning in life. They saw themselves as victims of history, with no sense of what a real man was to be.

If you fall into this historical grid as a Third-World man and want to rediscover your true manhood and the dignity of what it is to be a male in God's divine order of creation, this book was written to help you do just that. Remember, your past is not your future, and you are not a victim of your history. I challenge you to embrace the joy, responsibility, and honor of being a male made in the image of God. You have an obligation to restore the true image of manhood and to establish a model for our sons of this new generation. It is now your time to be proud to be a Third-World man.

The first-world man of Europe has failed to present the picture of the true man of God's image. The second-world man of the New World and industrial revolution has also failed to present the original image of God's man. Now you are the last world, the final world, the Third World. It is your turn to rediscover the original meaning of what it is to be a real man and to represent the image of God to a world that is in desperate need of a male prototype who will also restore purpose to the female and to children. It is your turn. Do it for our children, and make a difference.

About the Author

Dr. Myles Munroe is an international motivational speaker, best-selling author, lecturer, educator, and consultant for government and business. Traveling extensively throughout the world, Dr. Munroe addresses critical issues affecting the full range of human, social, and spiritual development. The central theme of his message is the transformation of followers into leaders and the maximization of individual potential.

Dr. Munroe is founder and president of Bahamas Faith Ministries International (BFMI), an all-encompassing network of ministries headquartered in Nassau, Bahamas. He is president and chief executive officer of the International Third World Leaders Association and the International Third World Leadership Training Institute. Dr. Munroe is also the founder, executive producer, and principal host of a number of radio and television programs aired worldwide and is a contributing writer for various Bible editions, magazines, and newsletters, including *The Believer's Topical Bible, The African Cultural Heritage Topical Bible, Charisma Life Christian Magazine,* and *Ministries Today.* He has earned degrees from Oral Roberts University and the University of Tulsa, and he was awarded an honorary doctorate from Oral Roberts University, for which he is an adjunct professor of the Graduate School of Theology.

Dr. Munroe and his wife Ruth travel as a team and are involved in teaching seminars together. Both are leaders who minister with sensitive hearts and international vision. They are the proud parents of two children, Charisa and Myles, Jr.

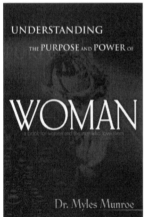

OTHER POWERFUL BOOKS

from Whitaker House

Even with My Issues
Dr. Wanda A. Turner

The enemy will try anything to prevent you from moving beyond your issues. But you can be free of the shame and bondage of your issues. Dr. Wanda Turner invites you on the most challenging journey you will ever take—a journey from rejection to acceptance, from fear to faith, from a shattered life to wholeness. Discover how you, too, can be entirely set free.

ISBN: 0-88368-673-2 • Trade • 160 pages

The Anatomy of God
Kenneth Ulmer

Throughout Scripture, God describes Himself in anatomical terms we are familiar with. His eyes wink and squint. His mouth whispers, His smile radiates, and He inclines an ear to our cries. In this book, Dr. Kenneth Ulmer introduces us to a God who is touchable, emotional, and accessible. If you desire to know God in a deeper way, or even if you question His closeness and concern, allow *The Anatomy of God* to draw to closer to Him.

ISBN: 0-88368-711-9 • Trade • 208 pages

Resolving Conflict in Marriage
Darrell Hines

Darrell Hines discusses the need for recognizing the spiritual forces that can destroy your marriage or keep it together. He identifies keys to preventing, confronting, and resolving conflict, and how you can find a place of agreement and move on. Discover today how you can begin walking together in the kind of relationship that overcomes trials and draws you together as never before.

ISBN: 0-88368-729-1 • Trade • 224 pages